New Zealand South Island

NZ FRENZY

SCOTT COOK

Scott Cook's Top-10 MUST-SEE South Island list:

Milford Sound drive (G20)
Mt Cook's Hooker Track (E5)
Franz Josef Glacier Walk (D7)
Rob Roy Glacier, Wanaka (G6)
Punakaiki Rocks (C8)
Queenstown's drives (G11, 12)
Curio Bay (F6)
Lake Tekapo's Mt John (E2)
Devil's Punchbowl Falls (B10)
Kaikoura Coast drive (A15)

**Cookie's favorite "off-the-beaten-path" outings
(in no order, as that'd be way too tough)**

Cave Stream (B7)
Halpins Falls (B9)
Monro Beach (D13)
Timaru Maori Art (E1)
Shag Pt boulders (E10)
Humboldt Falls (G16)
Clifden cave (F9)
Charming Creek (C4)
Haumuri Bluffs (A16)

Motukiekie Beach (C11)
Moeraki penguins (E9)
Amethyst hot pool (D4)
Wharariki/Pillar Pt (A2)
Cape Foulwind/Holcim's (C6)
Sawcut Gorge (A13)
Shadow Basin/ Lake Alta (G11)
Rawhiti Cave (A3)
Oparara Arches (C2)

Be sure to check FLICKR for color photos, maps, and additional info.

D1377774

The best place to get this book within New Zealand is at the 9 *Bivouac Outdoor* shops, or from their online store. Check www.bivouac.co.nz, search NZ Frenzy.

South Island New Zealand: NZ Frenzy
ISBN: 978-0-9799232-65
First Edition 2010
Copyright © 2010 by Scott Cook

All text and photography done by the author, except where noted.

Book design and layout by Jody Conners and Gary Asher, Maverick Publications, Bend, Oregon, USA.

Reach me: Scott Cook
              PO Box 861
              Hood River, Oregon, USA 97031
              Email: NzFrenzy@yahoo.com

FLICKR SITE::
WWW.FLICKR.COM/PHOTOS/NZFRENZY

Cover photo: Hooker Valley Track leading to Mt. Cook (E5)

Warning: Walking and tramping in New Zealand can be dangerous. All information within this book has been personally checked by the author to be accurate. However, track conditions can change. The author accepts no responsibility for any inconvenience or injury due to the use of this guide.

CONTENTS

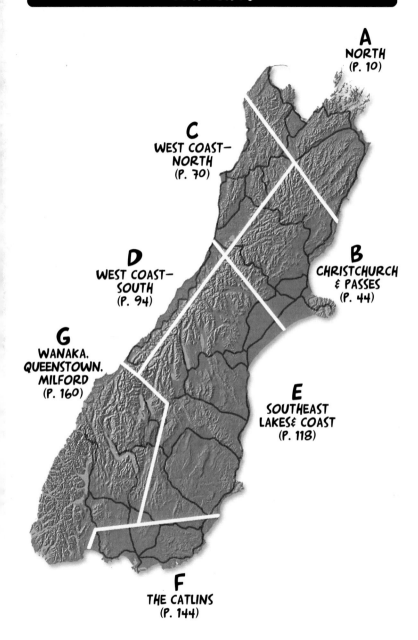

A
NORTH
(P. 10)

C
WEST COAST–
NORTH
(P. 70)

B
CHRISTCHURCH
& PASSES
(P. 44)

D
WEST COAST–
SOUTH
(P. 94)

G
WANAKA.
QUEENSTOWN.
MILFORD
(P. 160)

E
SOUTHEAST
LAKES& COAST
(P. 118)

F
THE CATLINS
(P. 144)

Base map courtesy of Geographx, Wellington, NZ

USING THIS GUIDE

READ THIS!!!!

My intention with NZ Frenzy is to help you have an absolutely fabulous visit to the South Island. Why I've researched and written this guide is because I find the available info within NZ frustratingly vague about the supposed "Real NZ"—the NZ that isn't all commercialized and brochured-to-death. Kiwi guidebooks are often short on the essential details needed to help a traveler choose how to spend their uber-valuable NZ time. Too often descriptions are vague, making your necessary decisions more difficult, as in *"Is It Worth It???"* Traveling in NZ you'll face decisions every single hour of every day…"should we do this, or that….go here, or there…check it out, or skip it." Often it's difficult to get detailed info about the next stops on your travel itinerary. The i-Sites may know a lot about their particular area, but they are most-often clueless about areas further away, thus making it difficult to budget your time. Questions like "Is Hanmer a two-hour stop, or two-day? Is Kaikoura just a boat trip, or is there much more? Is Dunedin a dull hour look-see, or a good base camp? Is there anything to do at Milford Sound except the boat tour?" This book is an attempt to help you speed-up and make better decisions for what, is for most people, their Once-in-a-Lifetime trip to New Zealand.

Flickr/Blog NZ Frenzy Websites. The first step to using this guide, in your planning stage, is to check-in with either my Flickr photo site or my NZ Frenzy Blog (the Blog may not be "live" until 2011). On these sites I'll post all the photos from the book, but at full size and color, plus add other photos that couldn't fit in print, but ones that I think are useful to give more of a feel for the particular area. Also, I've spent heaps of time labeling the trails and highlight points onto Google Earth maps in an attempt to further clarify outing in question. **The way I see it, these Google Maps may be this guide's best feature!** I've spent 5 years in NZ being confused by DOC literature about where particular trails leads and if the venture seems worth it. Thus I've made these maps with the special intent to clarify the essential info and details that the mainstream tourism media seems to leave frustratingly vague. All these maps are download-able. Feel free to save them onto your computer/iPhone or just print out the ones you may need. Also, when you are in NZ and begin to figure out your personal travel tastes—whether you want more "greatest hits" or yearn to escape the tourist crowds…then you can check back in with my sites to refresh your memory about the next destination in mind. I sincerely hope these maps help you out. They are what I wish I had when I was making my first forays to these fabled locations, because more often than not it took me hours to separate "the wheat from the chaff" and get going after consulting with i-Sites, guidebooks, and DOC pamphlets.

The Flickr address is **www.FLICKR.com/photos/NZfrenzy**. The Blog address is yet-to-be-determined, so just Google "NZFrenzyBlog" to see if I've had the time to get it going yet.

Hiking/Walking/Tramping in NZ. In NZ hiking is often called tramping, but also simply "walking", as in the "Great Walks." Also, there are no trails, but rather "tracks"…you tramp on a track rather than hike on a trail. In each entry, in the top box, I try to describe whether the track is a "walk" or a "tramp", because they are far different. When Kiwis describe a track as a Walk, they mean the track is maintained as a recognizable path with signage and switchbacks and such. Tramping tracks, on the other hand, often require scrambling of many sorts. On tramps you may find areas of complete wash-out that you have to rock-hop, rocky slopes that require full hands-on clambering, and many unbridged stream crossings. Sometimes there are even helper-ropes or chains to negotiate some tough spots. If I refer to a track as a tramp, then know that it requires a high level of gung-ho-ness. By way of comparison, an NZ "Walk" would be like a typical USA National Park trail, whereas a tramping track is more like a minor outdoor obstacle-course (which USA parks would close-off as too dangerous).

All walks and tramps in NZ are marked in some way with either plastic orange arrow-markers nailed to trees, or some sort of painted posts to show the route. These orange markers often lead across private farm plots (paddocks) to get to the track in the forest/beach/meadow. This system works well—I love following DOC's arrows!

Track signage in NZ often gives you a time estimate rather than a distance. You'll see a destination listed as "Lake Obvious, 90 minutes" rather than a distance to the lake. Loop tracks are often listed as "High loop, 2 hours return." Thus, "return" means round-trip. Rarely will any distance be given, and rarely do any of the tracks take nearly the recommended time for a reasonably fit hiker. The times that I list in the top box are all **My Personal Walking Times**. I timed every track at a walking pace, taking pictures and all that. It turns out that my walking times are consistently 60% of the general DOC estimate. If the sign says "one hour", I learned that for me it is 36 minutes. All too many times when I was new in NZ I skipped tracks and sights because I thought they'd take too long. I walk faster than most folks, but I do stop, gawk, and photo like everyone else. I hope that, at least, my times will be a consistent contrast to DOC's estimate, a sort of "real-world" gauge. Further, the DOC signs rarely have any distance indicated, and the distances I list are <u>estimates</u> based on two things: my walking pace and a track—distance <u>estimate</u> via Google Earth. FYI, my pace is roughly 5km/hour.

Obscur-O-Meter. The Obscurometer at the top of every entry is an attempt to gauge an outings' popularity, from a traveler's perspective. This is a subjective measure solely based upon my personal research and experience, and for the most part it's a summertime gauge during tourist season. Even Punakaiki is lonely in the Kiwi winter!

If an outing is skewed towards Obscure, then know that you probably won't find it written-up in the mainstream guidebooks, find much info via the i-Sites, nor street sign pointers. These Obscurometer gauges are meant to be an how-off-the-beaten-track shorthand. If the arrow is pinned to the left, expect nobody around but you and maybe a local…pinned to the right expect busloads of tourists. On the South Island the tourism paths are pretty well beaten, so I hope this gauge can help give you a "head's up" about upcoming possibilities. Personally, if I expect a crowd at an attraction, then the crowd doesn't bother me and I can enjoy the international tourism zoo….but if the media contrives to portray an attraction as "uncrowded and 100% pure" and I arrive and find the tourist hordes, then I'm often bitterly disappointed. Hopefully my Obscurometer will guide you to many many wonders that lie off the beaten track! Say hi to Taniwha for me (E1)!!

WATCH. "Meet The Locals" videos are fantastic bite-sized videos made jointly by TV NZ and the Dept of Conservation (DOC). Each one is a professionally-made 4-minute showcase of some part of NZ's natural world. To watch the one I list, just Google "Meet the Locals" and the video name.

For YouTube videos, enter the video code in the top YouTube search box. I've chosen these particular YouTube videos to try to help you plan your NZ trip. Of course you could zoom around YouTube for days looking at NZ stuff, but most of it is crap. Thus, I've waded through the crap to try to pick out videos which will really help you gain good insight into a location. Sometimes I looked long and hard to turn up some nuggets that weren't labeled very well. I'm not trying to spoil your surprise when you arrive at a new spot, but rather I'm trying to make sure you have enough info to plan your time wisely. When you see the vids for Ohau Falls (A14), Moeraki penguins (E9), and Curio's Hectors (F6)...I think you'll know what I mean. It is fun to chance upon stuff all by yourself...but it sucks worse to pass something by and have travelers at the next camp tell you about the "wonder you just missed". I'm pretty sure, armed with my book, you'll be the one telling other travelers what they've missed. Good on ya!!!!

Bring. Duh. I've been there before. Often I had wished some of the other guidebooks had given me this type of feet-on-the-ground advice....but they don't...I do.

Pronunciation. While I'm no cunning linguist, I do figure I can help you learn to pronounce some of the tricky Maori place names, so Wanaka is "wanna-ka" instead of "wa-nacka". Hope it helps.

NZ Sandflies. Here's a "head's up" to read the Sandfly appendix (App #1), before you get eaten.

Freedom Camping. Readers of my North Island book know that every entry listed some freedom camping options nearby. While that might work on the less-touristy North, it definitely doesn't apply to the South Island! In the past handful of years Freedom camping by travelers has become a very contentious hot-button issue on the South. Most of the problem results from too many van/car campers trying to all camp in the same few areas, namely Queenstown, Wanaka, the West Coast Road, Abel Tasman areas, and even downtown Christchurch. Plainly put, there just aren't enough nooks and crannies on the South to overnight in a car/van as there are on the North, and there are far more travelers attempting to squeeze into these fewer spots. As I write this there are new fines being enacted in many districts and "summit meetings" being held by industry leaders to try to remedy the localized problems, all while trying not to give NZ Tourism some kind of black-eye.

My advice for the South island is to be prepared to utilize local campgrounds and DOC sites. Get the DOC campground pamphlet. Get the campground/Holiday Park brochure maps. Then, use my Obscurometer to gauge the popularity of where you are heading—you won't be able to "park-up" near anywhere on the Popular side, but if the outing is more Obscure, then maybe you can "ask a local" if there are any known overnighting spots nearby. Don't mess up the pristine South Island by pooing in the bushes. If you're a cheap-o, then simply skip one expensive pay-for Kiwi "adventure" and save the money to pay a few more camping fees. The convenient campervan industry in NZ is super traveler-friendly, so don't ruin it for everyone and destroy the campervan industry by being insensitive to the local Kiwi concerns.

Advice for the author. This guidebook is far from perfect....no guidebook is right for everyone. But, I'd like to hear what you think so I can make it better and more useful to future NZ travelers. Write some notes on the following page...jot down any errors I've made or info you'd have wished for. When you get home please email me if you feel so inclined. I'd love the feedback, especially in areas that you think that I've been weak. I'm trying to help travelers squeeze the most out of their NZ time, so if I've misled you, I want to know. If you have nothing but praise, then yes I'd like to know, but a more useful place for it is on Amazon.com reviews or TripAdvisor.com or such. Thanks in advance, I'll appreciate your help.

Email: NZFrenzy@yahoo.com

Cheers,

NOTES TO TELL SCOTT:

AUTHOR'S NOTE

This is often the most difficult part of the book for me to write. This book has been 5 NZ summers in the making. I've just spent 5 USA winters/NZ summers of my life having the most wonderful times buzzing around New Zealand discovering one off-the-beaten-track wonder after the next. That was the Fun part!! In Feb 2010 I finally finished getting all my pictures and re-visiting all the places that the weather didn't cooperate with before. I got done cursing the rain, cursing the sandflies, and cursing the tourists. I've now spent the past 4 months in front of this computer trying to take my accumulated NZ knowledge and package it in a way that'll help YOU and future NZ travelers make the most of their NZ time. It's definitely not easy to winnow down a massive pile of South Island info into a concise, helpful, insightful guidebook. I can't put everything in, or the book becomes, in my opinion, unwieldy and less spot-on useful. It's sort of like distilling. The mainstream guidebooks, Kiwi books, i-Sites, and DOC pamphlets all have large volumes of tasteless and watered-down info which I then gather, test, and purify down into the book you're now holding—a high-proof NZ guidebook!

I hope you can appreciate my attempt to go the extra mile on every outing, giving you the essential details needed to have the best possible experience. I understand you are on a tight schedule in NZ with way too many options for however much travel time you have. I hope that my book can "cut through the clutter" of vague NZ info and give you the details and directions that are so-often lacking from the mainstream sources. I want my book to help you plan a good NZ route, but more so, I want my book to give you good quick options when your plans change due to weather, time, or whatever. Sooooo many tourists simply wander around NZ missing the best little bits because they have no good info at their fingertips. I don't want you to be them. Be at Punakaiki at high tide, be at penguin-viewing at 6pm, be on the beach walks at low tide, be in the hot springs after dark! These are the details and insights a savvy traveler needs. I hope that's why you bought this book, and I hope that I succeed in helping you have the BEST New Zealand trip EVER!!!!

Secondly, this author's note is difficult to write because it means I'm done writing this guidebook and now I have to market it. Self-publishing is tricky, but I think it makes for a better guidebook. I <u>need</u> to go the extra mile because I have no international reputation and marketing to fall back on. If I've failed and my book doesn't work for you, then I've spent years and tons of travel dollars for nothing (well, except for getting intimate with the planet's most amazing landscape! At least I've got that going for me, and that's not bad ☺) You've purchased this book, so obviously something I've done has worked. But, I need your help. If you like this guidebook, if it helped you have a killer trip, if you appreciate the "extra miles" I went to try to improve your trip, then I ask for your help. I need you to review NZ Frenzy on Amazon or talk it up on travel websites. If I've helped you have the NZ trip-of-a-lifetime, then please take a moment and help me. Without good reviews my book is worthless. Amazon.com is the only place I sell this book, and I imagine the only reason you purchased the book is because of the 5-star reviews. Please review me...and maybe email me. I sincerely appreciate hearing from NZ travelers who'll give me their opinions about my book—**the good and the bad. Write nzfrenzy@yahoo.com**

Hopefully with your help I'll sell heaps of books and become hyper-rich....and then invite everyone to a huge party! I'll rent-out all Fiordland, fly in the penguins, dolphins, keas, and all the cute baby seals from Ohau Falls.... and then heli everyone to the top of Key Summit for a NZ Frenzied bash that'll rock the Sounds!! See you there??

About the author: I'm 45, single, and live in the Shangri-La known as Oregon's Columbia River Gorge. I exclusively write guidebooks for a living nowadays, though I have no journalistic background whatsoever. In college I studied Math and Psychology. Since college I worked a corporate job for 7 years and have had "no real job" for the past 16 years. I like to kitesurf, mountain bike, hike, swim in lakes, jump in waterfalls, bask in hot springs... have a good time ☺.

You're holding my future in your hands...literally. If this guidebook works, then I can explore more and write more. Who wants to see Tasmania...who's up for Cape Town?

A

MAPS ON FLICKR ... CHECK THEM OUT!!

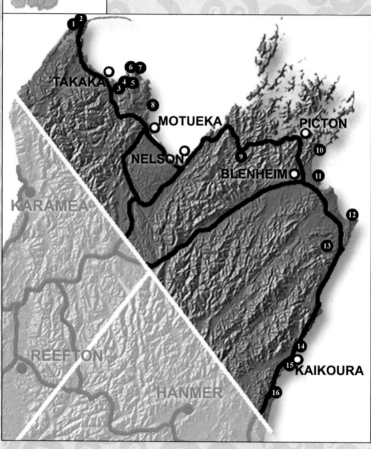

A1 Wharariki Beach
A2 Cape Farewell/Pillar Pt
A3 Rawhiti Cave
A4 The Grove
A5 Wainui Falls
A6 Wainui Bay/Taupo Pt
A7 Abel Tas. North – Anapai/Mutton Bays
A8 Marahau, Abel Tasman south walk

A9 Pelorus Bridge Scenic Reserve
A10 Port Underwood Drive
A11 Shipwreck of the SS Waverley
A12 Marfells Beach/Cape Campbell
A13 Sawcut Gorge
A14 Ohau Pt/Waterfall
A15 Kaikoura
A16 Haumuri Bluffs

NORTH REGION

The north bit of the South is a varied landscape with a scattering of unique natural attractions. Nelson is the main city that attracts traveler interest, but even though Nelson does have great weather, a fun vibe, and a gorgeous location, there are actually not too many places of interest in Nelson – everything is a substantial drive away. The Marlborough Sounds offer some off-the-beaten-track opportunities, but expect slow windy roads and scenery more sublime than dramatic. The Marlborough wine country surrounding Blenheim receives increasing international acclaim for its wines. The spot on the north that gets the most Tourism hoopla is the famed Abel Tasman Nat'l Park and Great Walk. The "AT" is NZ's most popular Great Walk, renowned for its beautiful beaches and beautiful weather. What the brochures fail to tell is that in the summer there isn't a drop of solitude anywhere near or on the AT Walk—expect the masses, as there is no escape. The AT is the most hustle-bustle of any of the Great Walks because the walkers are joined by kayakers and a flotilla of shuttle boats and their tourists.

Golden Bay hosts an impressive array of outdoor delights. The main town of Takaka suffers none of the busy-ness of Motueka/Kaiteriteri/Marahau. Takaka is a mellow town, the masses kept at bay by the steep and windy access road over Takaka Hill. The vast majority of NZ tourists get their Abel Tasman fix on the southern end of the Great Walk instead of venturing north up the "dead-end" SH 60. Don't be one of those masses – check out Golden Bay! (FYI, the DOC Totaranui Camp at the north end of the AT is packed with campers all summer long—don't imagine that it may be an out-of-the-way gem—no way!)

Kaikoura, down the east coast along a GORGEOUS stretch of seaside highway, is NZ's whale-watch/marine life capitol. Twenty years ago Kaikoura was a town in danger of dying until the local Maoris pooled their money to begin Whale Watch Kaikoura. This whale-watch operation has been a smashing success, literally putting Kaikoura "back on

the map". There are no whales to see from the town or beaches, so if you want to whale-watch (or dolphin or seal), be prepared to pay for a boat ride. Even if whale-watching isn't in the budget, a visit to Kaikoura is definitely worth it. The drive is stunning—the best coastal drive anywhere in NZ...the seal colonies are raucous and the walking opportunities are uber-scenic. Kaikoura is a gem!

Watch: Meet the Locals: "Abel Tasman" and "Kaikoura"

Don't Miss:
  Abel Tasman's north side (7)
  Wharariki Beach/Pillar Pt (1, 2)
  Golden Bay (3-7)
  Kaikoura (15)

A1 ▶ WHARARIKI BEACH
(fara-rickey)

STUNNING BEACH SCENERY!!

**Walk: moderate 1.0km walk to beach
  with 5km loop option**

• watch YouTube: xt2_wkfwca4
• bring: headlamps (for caves), sandals

OBSCURE   POPULAR
OBSCUR-O-METER

Wharariki Beach is arguably the most impressive and intriguing beach on the South Island. Wharariki is <u>definitely unlike</u> any other beach on the South Island. Compared to Abel Tasman's bright and inviting beaches, Wharariki is dark and mysterious. Abel's beaches are like a pretty cheerleader, whereas Wharariki's beckon like a moody, tattooed and tempestuous woman.

Archway Islands

People ◀

The Wharariki Beach itself is about a mile-long cove bookended by rocky headlands. In between the headlands, well,…it's as if Mother Nature picked up a handful of beautiful beachscape features—dunes, rocks, caves, arches, sea stacks, and islands—gathered them up and tossed them across Wharariki's cove like dice, leaving them scattered in every direction. Sort of like an orgy—good stuff just piled up! The just-offshore Archway Islands are uber-scenic with sheer rock faces and archway holes…the dunes dazzle with an array of windswept patterns…and the rocks studding and bookending the beach are laced with caves and a myriad of thru-passages—bring a headlamp, as some of the passages are so long that you'll want extra light!!

Two things to know: this beach is notoriously windy, and thus the sand dunes. But, the constant wind means NO SANDFLIES—Yay! Wharariki might be the sole West Coast beach without a sandfly plague. Bring extra clothes because it's way windier at the beach than the carpark. Try to visit at half-tide or lower, because at higher tides you can't access many of the labyrinthine tunnels and archways.

Wharariki is literally the end of the road from Golden Bay, but it still sees about 50 visitors per summer day. Most visitors are lazy though and

Stone Bridge

**Stone Bridge Beach
(South Wharariki)**

often don't walk the entire beach all the way to the south end of the long cove to Stone Bridge Beach. Make sure you do—the south end is the most impressive!

Walk There is a mapboard at the carpark showing the tracks. From the carpark there are a couple of options, the first being the 12-minute "Hilltop Walk" over the hills to the beach. If the wind is howling from the west, Dion (the campground owner), recommends that people walk the more-protected farm track south/west first, cross the paddock to the "Stone Bridge beach", then walk back up the entire beach with the wind at your back (the Hilltop walk is marked at the top of the big dunes…if you got to the creek you're a bit too far).

If you want to investigate an even more remote beach, then the signed Green Hill Beach is another 25 minute walk along the paddock track from the Stone Bridge Beach track. Chances are there'll be nobody but you at this isolated (though less-scenic) cove (from carpark to Green hill beach is a 35-minute walk).

FYI There is a new campground/Holiday Park at Wharariki Beach which opened in Feb 2010, and thus may not yet be in some guide-books. It costs a few dollars more, but the hot showers to wash off the windy salt and sand spray are worth it! Spending a sunset at Wharariki is divine! Check www.WhararikiBeachHolidayPark.co.nz.

DRIVING: Wharariki is about 60km from Takaka, about an hour's drive. Head towards Farewell Spit on SH 60 and after passing tiny Port Puponga, turn left at the last sign before Farewell Spit, then go 5km of gravel to Wharariki's road-end carpark.

A2 ▶ CAPE FAREWELL/PILLAR POINT LIGHTHOUSE TRACK
DRAMATIC HEADLANDS ROUTE

Walk: moderate 8-9 km loop
- elevation carpark: 15m
- elevation lighthouse: 150m
- watch YouTube: bv72r4kpc-e

OBSCURE · POPULAR
OBSCUR-O-METER

The 5km one-way headlands walk from Wharariki Beach carpark to the Pillar Point Lighthouse is possibly the most dramatic headlands walk on the South Island! This is an exceptional route—nowhere else on the South's West coast is there a walk as cliffy and interesting as this.

The views of the cave-studded, striped and eroded cliffs are magnificent the entire way, and then the lighthouse views over the entire Farewell Spit and Golden Bay add 100% more. Halfway along the route is the actual Cape Farewell (which you can also drive to or use to shorten the loop.) The Cape is must-see for any Wharariki visitor. The Cape view-platform overlooks a dramatic cliff, to say the least! Down below seals lounge on the rocks and waves bash up a monster spray. Just west (south) of the actual cape you'll get a bird's eye view down into an inlet hosting a Fur Seal breeding colony where the pups often can be seen frolicking in the surf. From the cape the route continues along the bluffs/hills to the lighthouse.

The finale of the route is the Pillar Point Lighthouse (also accessible by a 20-minute walk from the roadside carpark). The lighthouse itself is bland, but the view is divine (especially 3 minutes farther!) The grey sands of Farewell Spit arc towards a horizon peppered with the mountains of the North Island. Golden Bay shines to the south with Abel Tasman's

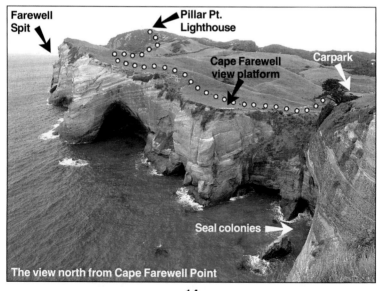

The view north from Cape Farewell Point

Separation Point being land's end of the Golden Bay. For fun guess which way is true north? To figure it out head back to the lighthouse, where the mounted solar panel faces just a few degrees west of true north. On a clear day the perfect cone of North Island's Mt Taranaki floats on the horizon about 45° east of north, just 100 miles away!

Seal pups

View down from Cape Farewell Point

Walk There is no actual "track" per se, but rather this is a route marked with colored poles that stays near the headlands cliffs most of the way from beach to lighthouse. Given that it's often super-windy, walking the route from beach to lighthouse is the more-pleasant direction. It's possible to make a loop out of the excursion by getting to the lighthouse then walking about 1.2km down its road, then going right on Wharariki Rd for 2.4km back to the carpark. Or, you can backtrack from the lighthouse to the Cape Farewell view-platform and then take the road back to the carpark 2km from there.

For a shorter loop you could drive to the Cape Farewell viewpoint and do a 5-ish km loop from there.

Farewell Spit seen from Pillar Pt. Lighthouse

DRIVING: Same as entry A1. Begin at the Wharariki carpark and mapboard.

A3 ▶ RAWHITI CAVE
(ra-fiddy)

A MILLION STALACTITES!

**Walk: Difficult 35-minutes to and into cave
(2km one-way)**

• watch YouTube: "Rawhiti Cave"
• bring: solid shoes, headlamp, tripod

OBSCUR-O-METER

Whoa! Nothing prepared me for the sight of the Rawhiti Cave opening, even though I had been told it was "impressive" a number of times. Rawhiti Cave is different than any other public cave in New Zealand. The cave is tricky to

describe, as it's not a tunnel-cave, but rather it's sort of a deep angling overhanging pit. Light penetrates way into this cave—thus there's no imperative need for a torch, but it's best to bring one anyway. The difficult marked path into the cave descends a rugged and slippery 50-60 meters down into the pit before abruptly ending at the lip of a black hole.

Cave opening

Thus far Rawhiti Cave may not sound too interesting…but here's the hook: roughly a million stalactites hang from the pit wall! The angling wall is literally covered with a mind-boggling array of drip-stone spikes ranging from grotesquely huge to small rows of crocodile teeth. The stalactites even show some odd coloration. Taking the path down inside you'll soon encounter a garden of massive stalagmites growing from the cave floor, surrounded by mounds of drip terraces. Oh my! So much light shines in from the yawning opening that the cave slope is festooned with ferns and

A million stalactites

mosses. Moss grows on the stalactites, and if you look close at the lower stalagmites you may notice that the moss grows at an angle to attempt to capture the most light possible. Intriguingly, the calcite-laden cave drips then trickle down the angling moss growth to create some rare cave weirdness—angling stalactites! Look up and notice how any stalactite exposed to the light has both moss and curvature—super unique!

If it's a grey day in Golden Bay, Rawhiti Cave is the place to be!

Walk/Tramp The track to the cave is a difficult 35-minute tramp. The first 15 minutes are easy paralleling the creekbed, but the next 20 minutes are super steep up the canyon wall to the cave opening. Then you descend the optional slippery slope into the cave abyss.

Stalagmite grove

DRIVING: In Takaka take the turn signed for Pohara/Totaranui for 5km. At the T-intersection known as "Butcher's Corner" go right for 400m then left onto Packard Rd. Follow Packard 2.7km then turn left at the Rawhiti Cave sign and follow the gravel road 1km through two gates and paddocks to the signed road-end carpark in the grassy paddock.

A4 ▶ THE GROVE

LIMESTONE BOULDER GARDEN JUNGLE

Walk: easy 30-minute loop (1.3 km)

● Golden Bay Must-See

OBSCURE • POPULAR
OBSCUR-O-METER

Nobody should visit Takaka without doing the short loop walk through The Grove. This is one of the best easy short walks on the entire South Island! Just a few minutes from Takaka, The Grove transports you into a mysterious Thailand-like jungly boulder garden. Basically there's just a short loop path touring an amazing limestone boulder wonderland with a surprise nook around each corner. Trees ooze onto the blocks, vines wrap from tree to boulder…palms tower overhead, ferns under… nooks, crannies, crevices… The Grove's got it all in just a 30-minute stroll!

Funky Palms

Vine-a-rama

FYI ▶ If you liked The Grove's limestone, then maybe pop into Takaka Recycling Centre's Labyrinth Rocks Park for a bit more limestone maze-walking.

DRIVING: In Takaka head for Pohara/Totaranui. Go 5 km of right zigzags until "Butcher's Corner"/Glenview Rd. Go left here towards Pohara for just 2km then turn right in Clifton at a sign for The Grove and zigzag another 1.0km to the signed carpark.

A5 ▶ WAINUI FALLS TRACK
(why-new-ee)

ABEL TASMAN AREA'S SOLE WATERFALL

Walk: moderate 25-minutes one-way (2km)

- bring: swimsuit, water shoes
- watch YouTube: n2mrekatdsu

OBSCUR-O-METER

Sunny waterfall

Wainui Falls is a fantastic waterfall! Fantastic riverside track, fantastic swingbridge, fantastic deep swimming-hole, fantastic smooth rocks for diving and sunning. Wainui's the best and most inviting waterfall on the northern bit of the South Island!

First off, the track to Wainui Falls is a joy as you amble upstream on the easy-ish track above the gurgling stream. You'll then cross a fun swingbridge before popping around a corner to find the waterfall. Whoa, Wainui Falls is about 20m high and gushes down a mossy cliff face into a deep sun-dappled pool. Just before plunging into the pool, the

Fun swingbridge

falls bonks full-force onto a protruding rock, causing a misty spray that adds a rainbow to the festivities. Bring a picnic and bring a swimsuit, as this is a waterfall that simply begs for a dip and a relaxing sun-dry. No better way to rinse off an Abel Tasman day than with a plunge into Wainui Falls' pool!

Wainui is super-popular, so expect other visitors, but the roar of the falls nicely drowns-out the other voices.

DRIVING: From Takaka head east towards Totaranui for 23km. Wainui Falls is signed at the far end of sweeping Wainui Bay. Turn right onto the gravel road to the carpark.

A6 ▶ WAINUI BAY/TAUPO POINT ROUTE
(why-new-ee)

OFF-THE-BEATEN-PATH ABEL TASMAN BEACHES

Walk: moderate 40-minute one-way (3km)

● bring: tide chart, water shoes

OBSCURE — POPULAR
OBSCUR-0-METER

Rare Abel Tasman solitude

This 40-minute beach/rocks/headlands route is like the "Abel Tasman" before the tourism invasion…more like when Abel first sighted the area in 1642, rather than the nowadays tourist-a-rama. This off-the-beaten-path route begins from the Wainui carpark—the true northern end of the Abel Tasman (AT) Track. Few AT walkers venture on the northern section of the track from Totaranui because it adds too much length and elevation and doesn't have any convenient shuttles or other A.T. hoopla. This out 'n' back route doesn't follow the AT, but instead branches off and hugs the coves on over to the NorthWesternMost point of the Abel Tasman headland group—Taupo Point. Few travelers walk this route as a day-walk, mostly because the AT draws all the attention away from anything else in the immediate area, leaving this little beach 'n' cove route mostly for locals and kayak-campers. The destination, Taupo Point, was once a Maori pa site and now is simple a lonely curve of golden sand…with some campspots and a toilet. One side of the point or the other will be calm enough to swim and frolic in the delightfully people-free Abel Tasman environs. The views are ALL of Golden Bay!

The route takes a little bit of planning, but not much. One hour on either side of high tide is when the route becomes a wet and slippery chore, but still do-abel. This route makes a good overnight quick backpack outing—all the sunny beaches, none of the "Great Walk" hut-bookings/plannings/crowds/homes/$$$s…more Tasman than tourism. You'll like it.

Walk Heading from the Wainui carpark, 15 minutes into the route, near the end of the first long beach, a signed "High Tide Route" leaves the beach to pop over the upcoming headland pinch spot—look sharp for the sign and path, cuz it's easy to miss as you're watching your steps over the rocks. The route then acends/decends to the next beach and then on to the isthmus at Taupo Point where you'll find the Maori-history plaque. The final beach is just steps away.

History plaque

DRIVING: From Takaka head towards Pohara/Totaranui. The signed Wainui carpark road is in 23km, immediately past the Wainui Falls road, on the northern end of Wainui Bay. Turn left to find the road-end carpark. A mapboard at the carpark shows the route.

A7 ABEL TASMAN NORTH –
THE ANAPAI/MUTTON BAYS TRACK

THE LESS-CROWDED SIDE OF THE ABEL TASMAN TRACK

Walk: moderate 1-2 hours one-way (3-6 km)

● Low tide is best—more beach!

OBSCUR-O-METER

The vast majority of Abel Tasman backpackers do the 3-day route from Marahau to Totaranui. The vast majority of day-walkers, shuttle-walkers, and day-kayakers swarm the Marahau section of the track because that's where all the commercialism is based. This bit of the AT, the northern corner of the park towards Separation Point, sees far fewer footsteps, yet its beaches and bush are just as inviting as any on the more popular route. Here's the deal: if you head south from Totaranui for a day walk you'll probably see 100 people (folks either ending/beginning the 3-day track or day-walkers from Totaranui campground), head north and you'll see maybe 20-30 people.

Walking the track for an hour to the north you'll get thick jungle, great ridge-top vistas, and four different stretches of wonderful Abel Tasman orange-sand beach—great bang-for-the-buck! This walk is FAR superior to the too-busy AT day walk north from Marahau!!

Anapai Bay

To Totaranui

Mutton Bay from AT Track

Walk Anapai Bay is first up after a 30-minute ascent/descent through a wondrous dense jungle. Anapai's got neat rocky nooks at either end and a small campsite in its middle. North from Anapai you'll pass a small unnamed cove and then ascend the headlands for 30 more minutes to Mutton Bay. From the track you'll get postcard-perfect views of both Anapai and Mutton. Mutton Bay is a two-for-one beach with a rocky outcrop splitting the beach into two halves. A beach walk, then a swim to the other beach for another walk…is well-done Mutton! (hahaha.) From Mutton the AT continues about 20 minutes more to the Separation Point Lighthouse. The lighthouse isn't too scenic, but there may be seals on the rocks and killer views of the entire Golden Bay and Spit. From Totaranui to the lighthouse

Mutton Bay seclusion

is about 90-120 minutes one-way, so it makes for a long day hike, but it's probably the best combo of scenery, beauty, and least crowding anywhere on the Abel!

DRIVING: From Takaka head towards Totaranui for 23km paved, then continue on the slow gravel for 11km more to the DOC Totaranui Campground/Abel Tasman trailhead (50 minutes from Takaka.) Entering the campground the track you want is immediately left, but first stop into the beachside DOC Centre to take a photo of the mapboard, etc.

23

A8 ▶ MARAHAU – THE ABEL TASMAN DAY WALK

FABLED (AND CROWDED) ABEL TASMAN DAY-WALK

Hike: easy/moderate 5-7 km one-way

● watch Meet the Locals: "Abel Tasman"

OBSCUR-O-METER

Abel Tasman Park is NZ's busiest National Park. The day walk on the Abel Tasman, north from Marahau, is one of the South Island's busiest walks. You've got all the backpackers heading both to and fro, day-walkers doing an out/back, and also plenty of one-way walkers who take a water taxi shuttle to either Bark Bay or Anchorage and then walk back. The day walk is easy the entire way as it contours through the bush about 50-70 meters above the coves. The most popular turnaround points are Apple Tree Bay (5km, 60-min one-way) or 20 minutes farther to Stilwell Bay (7.2km, 80 min).

Apple Tree Bay

Overall, this walk isn't too remarkable compared to the high expectation Tourism Abel sets with all its "no-people and perfect low-tide 'n' sunshine" pix. Most of the day-walk is through unremarkable bush with few views of either sea or beach coves. The two turnaround beaches are often crowded with both walkers as well as a flotilla of lunching kayakers. Expect zero solitude. The beaches are hardly noteworthy, especially at high tide when they all but disappear (and Stilwell only reachable via a waist-deep wade). Oh, both Apple Tree and Stilwell haves houses on them, adding to that "special" feeling the brochures somehow leave out.

But, here are some tips for having a good time on this walk. First, <u>Bring a Swimsuit!</u> Abel's waters are both the calmest and warmest on the South, so if you don't take a dip here, you may never will. Stilwell Bay has some small islands easily reached via a swim/wade (my favorite time was

High tide at Stilwell Bay

Swim

Wade to beach

when I swam over and climbed onto the rocks just in time to see a meter-wide ray glide by!) At Apple Tree a lagoon channel divides the beach. If you wade the channel to keep walking you'll get a sense of solitude until you come to the two houses. Past the houses, where the sands widen, there's a hidden path that heads up the slope with the help of a garden hose to regain the track, thus making an Apple Tree beach mini-loop. Finally, on the return route, pop down 2 minutes to Coquille Bay. Coquille is the best low-tide beach on the route, yet few people visit because they're either too close to the start or "over it" and tired on the way back. Coquille is just 30-minutes from the track start. If you have any urge to skinny-dip the A.T., the secluded north end of Coquille may be your best bet.

A much better day walk on the A.T. is at the north end, heading north from Totaranui (entry A7).

One Marahau highlight not to miss is the *"Arts Unique"* sculpture emporium located at the trailhead car-park—the carvings there are epic!

Coquille Beach low tide

DRIVING: Marahau is signed on SH 60 a few kms north of Motueka. Just keep driving around the bay and past the waterfront until you get to the large signed DOC trailhead carpark where there are toilets and route mapboards.

A9 ▶ PELORUS BRIDGE SCENIC RESERVE

SWIMMING HOLE RIVER

Walk: various walks

- nice DOC campground
- watch YouTube: _tow9zdn_ky

OBSCUR-O-METER
OBSCURE POPULAR

The Pelorus Scenic Reserve is a total off-the-beaten-path gem, at least by foreign traveler standards. Locals know it and LOVE it…travelers zoom past without a clue. What you've got here is the crystal-clear Pelorus River lazily winding through one of the South Island's most-accessible stands of virgin forest. Even better, the Pelorus pools up into some inviting swimming holes rimmed by oh-so-dive-able rocks…and even better-better, the Pelorus is about the warmest river water you're gonna find anywhere on the South Island. If you're unwilling to dive into the deep, clear, warmish water of the Pelorus, then chances are that you'll never swim anywhere on the South Island. And, to make the whole shebang even more enticing, there's a $10 DOC campground onsite with HOT showers and a café for the hungry and thirsty. Thus, THERE'S NO REASON, NOT EVEN DOWNPOUR RAIN, NOT TO STOP AND JUMP INTO 100% PURE NEW ZEALAND!!!!!!!!!!!!!!!!!!!

As if that's not enough, there are nice walking tracks in the Pelorus Reserve for every level of energy and fitness. Easy tracks lead to a massive Totara tree and an 80m swingbridge spanning the neighboring Rai River, while a moderate loop track gains 350m in 2.5km up to K Trig. This place is New Zealand. This place isn't in Lonely Planet.

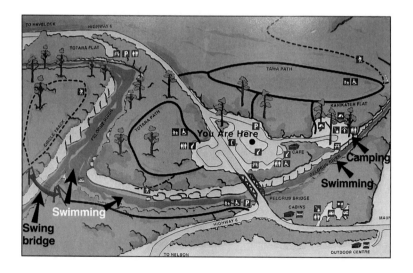

FYI Going to or from the Picton Ferry takes about 60 minutes from Pelorus, so it makes a great first or last night on the South!

Walk The carpark mapboard shows all the tracks. The K Trig track is almost worthless, as are the trickling "waterfalls". There's no view from the Trig worth seeing...so the only reason to do the 45-minute roundtrip track is simply for a good work-out. All the easy short walks are nice.

DRIVING: Pelorus is located about 45 minutes from Nelson (55km) or 60 minutes from Picton (49km). It's 19km west of Havelock, obviously signed on SH6.

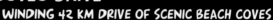

A10 ▷ PORT UNDERWOOD ROAD BEACH COVES DRIVE

WINDING 42 KM DRIVE OF SCENIC BEACH COVES

Walk: moderate 1-hour viewpoint track at White's Bay

● bring: patience, sunshine

OBSCUR-O-METER
OBSCURE — POPULAR

Robin Hood Bay from road

Camp

Road

This is the slow road to Picton from Blenheim for those who want to savor the South Island just a little more before heading North (coming South from the ferry most folks are too amped up to get to Nelson/Golden Bay or Kaikoura to enjoy this slow leisurely delight.) This 42 km road (about two hours drive) from Rarangi Beach to Picton is one of the windingest on the island—and half of its length is unsealed, but still a good road. Make no mistake, this road is slow as it visits a handful of intimate coves and then rises up to skirt the view-packed headlands in between. But the sights are plenty and you'll DEFINITELY be OFF the tourist track…and you'll get a taste of driving one of Marlborough Sounds' super-curvy roads, but this one actually delivers you to a new place, rather than the out/ back chores that are that are the Queen Charlotte and Pelorus roads. If you've got a ferry booked, then maybe make this your final venture on the South Island. If you camp at DOC's Whatamango Bay, then Picton is just an easy 15-minute drive, making the Port Underwood Rd drive a slow peaceful farewell to one of the most amazing places in the world—the South island of New Zealand.

Here's the rundown on attractions and options, listed south to north:

Rarangi Beach: $6 DOC campground on a looong shingle (pebble) beach. At north end of beach is a staircase over to cute little sandy Monkey Bay. At the staircase the plaque details Daddy Watson's cave—bring a torch and have a look—it's directly in front of the plaque in the bush—and it goes in a surprising 60-70 meters and sports a few glow worms.

Port Underwood/Sounds

Road

North

Whites Bay. About 6km north of Rarangi, and this first 6km is typical of the up/down on the entire route (but the seal ends at Whites for the next 20km to Oyster Bay.) Whites Bay has a spacious, yet sheltered, $6 DOC camp with toilets and showers. There are also a couple of walking tracks and an explorable beach arch. The best track is Black Jack Lookout loop which is a steady uphill of 25 minutes to the view, then 20 back down (left at the upper junction). From the viewpoint you'll see Cape Palliser, Port Underwood, and probably a ferry making the crossing.

Robin Hood Bay. The biggest and sandiest bay on the route, but still intimate. Free Doc camp on south side with heaps of day-use parking along the entire bay front. Toilets on either end. Low-tide tide pools are fun to explore.

Ocean Bay/Bob Canes Bay. Small coves with water access, but no sandy beaches. Bob Canes has waterside picnic grounds. Neither is too exciting.

Oyster Bay. The road becomes sealed here again for the drive up over the hill towards the Sounds and Picton. Oyster Bay has some cottages and a wharf/boatramp, but nothing too scenic for travelers. From here the road leaves Port Underwood and climbs the hill over to the Sounds, with a good pull-off view-stop at the top of the grade.

Whatamango Bay. Large $6 basic DOC camp on an arm of the Sounds. Good kayaking. Nice place for the first/last night on the island.

Marlborough Sounds

North Island

Port Underwood Lookout

Whites Bay

29

A11 ▶ SHIPWRECK OF THE SS WAVERLEY

EASY WALK TO SHIPWRECK RUINS

Walk: easy 80-minute loop (7 km)

OBSCURE · POPULAR
OBSCUR-O-METER

Surprisingly, the best and most accessible shipwreck remains on the entire South Island are in Blenheim's Wairau Lagoon. The only other visible shipwreck is the hard-to-see "Ino" near the Catlins' Fortrose town (entry F7). Hokitika trumpets a shipwreck replica, but it hardly captivates more than a moment's attention. But the SS Waverley has both a story and ruins worth seeing, if you've got an unhurried 2 hours to spend here.

Before describing the wreck though, here are the details of the walk to it. The DOC sign says "3 hours return" for the loop walk to the wreck. Hardly! The walk is the flattest walk on the entire South—dead flat the whole way along the banks of the Wairau lagoon. Go counter-clockwise...the longer route takes 46 minutes at a fast walk...while the shorter return only takes 33 minutes—(1hr, 20 minutes...not 3 hours. 7km total loop.)

Now, the story of the wreck: The Waverley is only a quasi-shipwreck. It was a steamer built in 1883 and saw its last service in 1928 carrying miners and supplies to the remote West Coast gold fields. In 1928 it was purposely dismantled and towed to the Wairau River mouth in order to be sunk there as part of a breakwater. But the weather fouled the scuttling and the Waverley floated into the lagoon and stranded where it now rests 80 years later.

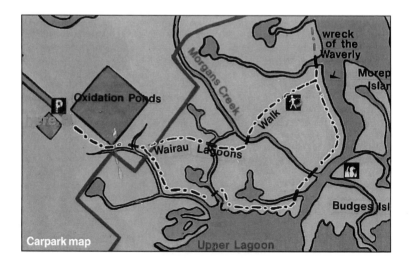

The wreck itself is somewhat picturesque— the rusting hulk contrasts nicely with a deep blue sky. And, the wreck sits in just inches of water, so it's fairly easy to step over to it (low tide is best to stay dry) and climb aboard! Of course the rusty hulk is dangerous and any mishap could mean sudden death or torturous gangrene... so you better just take a photo.

Inside the Waverley

DRIVING: From the Blenheim i-Site head 6km south towards Kaikoura on SH 7. Turn left onto Hardings Rd signed to Wairau Lagoon and go 3km to the road-end carpark.

A12 MARFELLS BEACH/CAPE CAMPBELL LIGHTHOUSE

BEACH WALK TO SCENIC LIGHTHOUSE

Walk: easy 80-minute one-way (7 km)

- bring: tide chart, water sandals
- Google: "Cape Campbell Lighthouse"

OBSCURE POPULAR
OBSCUR-O-METER

Marfells Beach is a long sandy beach with views over Clifford/Cloudy Bay to the distant North Island mountains. One of the best aspects of Marfells Beach is that it sports a beachside DOC campground—perfect for sunrises and long low-tide beach walks. Expect a FULL campground at Xmas/New Years.

DOC Campground

Marfells Beach is probably the best beach walking anywhere near Blenheim and the NE bit of the South. Most every beach near Blenheim is pebbly and tough walking, but Marfells has long expanses of hard-packed sand, perfectly suited to a long contemplative beach walk. Better yet, Marfells beach has a perfect destination for this long beach walk—the South Island's eastern-most lighthouse at Cape Campbell. The lighthouse is a <u>long</u> steady walk of 80 minutes (7km), one-way. Most of the walk is on solid packed sand—making for easy walking, but there are sections where you'll have to clamber over some shoreline rocks. The tide is an issue here—a falling tide is the best time to make the long out/back to the lighthouse. The "pinch-point" rocks, the most difficult to get around as the tide rises, are those between Marfells and the nearby point—Mussell Point. Thus, since the trip will take 3 hours (minimum), it's on the way back that a

Approaching Cape Campbell

rising tide will bite you and make you pick your way high over some rough rocks to (hopefully) elude the waves. There is a DOC campground host on site at Marfells Beach who can fill you in on tide-timing details and route planning.

The lighthouse is a worthy goal (there is no <u>public</u> road access to it… you have to walk!) It was built in 1905 and a plaque details its history.

1905 lighthouse

Arriving at the site you'll pass the oft-empty care-taker residence and then climb the 91 stairs to the sweeping view. Pack a lunch, drinks, binoculars, and your NZ atlas map… so you can both search for whale spout and identify all the bits of the North Island that are plain to see on a clear day.

Hike 20 minutes to Mussell Point—a good short walk where you'll get at least a look to the far cape and lighthouse. From Mussell it's a solid hour more…just you and the waves and the scenic cliffs.

DRIVING: Head south from Blenheim on SH1 for 36km. Marfells Beach Rd is signed on the south side of Lake Grassmere. Turn and go 8km of gravel to the seaside campground. (The DOC camp is $6pp, directly on the beach).

A13 ⟩ SAWCUT GORGE STREAMBED ROUTE

NZ'S FINEST SLOT CANYON

**Tramp: streambed route 40 minutes (3 km)
one-way to Sawcut Gorge**

● Google: "Sawcut Gorge"

OBSCURE · POPULAR
OBSCUR-O-METER

Note: this is a sunny-day route. Do not attempt the route just after a huge rainstorm.

This in-the-streambed route leads to Sawcut Gorge, NZ's finest slot canyon. Surprisingly, this slot canyon was featured on i-Site's 2010 brochure cover (but without identifying it as Sawcut Gorge—most of NZ's i-Sites had no idea how to "put you there"). The "Sawcut" itself is a short and narrow slot-canyon passage where Isolation Creek has eroded through a 50m-high wall of limestone, leaving a unique slot that's higher than it is long. Sawcut Gorge is as impressive as the famed slots of Utah's canyon country, but, sadly, it's fairly short.

That said, the fun of this outing is more than just seeing the short slot canyon. The entire route leading to the Sawcut is a fun splashing tromp up the shallow Waima River for about 40 minutes. The marked DOC route criss-crosses the stream innumerable times with paths along the banks to avoid deep spots. The water is warmish in the summer and mostly ankle-to-knee deep. Mid-day is the best time to venture up to see the Sawcut—the noon sun will glimmer on all the deep emerald swimming holes, whereas in the late afternoon the shadows can make the route much chillier.

In the Waima River

Tramp Walk down the road from the house and then begin up the stream. The entire route is in the streambed and marked by DOC arrows. Water shoes are a must! After 30 minutes the gorge narrows as the walls begin to tower. Just past a small right-side waterfall the route goes up on the right bank for a short time to avoid a deep boulder-pinched spot. Soon after this pinch you'll see the Isolation Reserve sign on the left side of the stream. Go left here on the marked path which cuts over into the Isolation Creek side-canyon where another 5-10 minutes upstream will yield the impressive Sawcut.

Sawcut Gorge

After the adventure through the Sawcut, it's possible to follow Isolation Creek another 30-ish minutes to a hut, but the route becomes a bit bland. Better is to head back to the Waima River and find a nice swimming and sunning spot at the Isolation Creek confluence or maybe slosh a bit more upstream in the Waima Canyon to find your own secret spot.

DRIVING: On SH 1, 8km south of Ward or 14 km north of Kekerengu, turn west onto Ure Rd just north of the signed Waima River bridge. From SH 1 it's a scenic 12km 2WD gravel road (about 20 minutes) to the DOC trailhead at the Blue Mountain Station homestead. Please leave the numerous gates as you found them. Arriving at the Blue Mountain home, the "official" parking is immediately in front of the private home in the angled spaces. Possibly the friendly station owners, Mr. & Mrs. Buick, will be there with a welcoming Kiwi greeting and a chat about the route. These charming Kiwis are happy to chat with what Mr. Buick says are the 3-8 average daily summertime visitors. Please sign their guest book on their veranda.

A14 ▶ OHAU POINT FUR SEALS
(o-how)

FUR SEAL PLAYGROUND

Walk: easy 5-minute walk

- watch YouTube: b3zazqqwowi
  & gjtc3jjd-eg

OBSCURE POPULAR
OBSCUR-O-METER

22 km north of Kaikoura on SH1 is signed Ohau Point and its resident Fur seal breeding colony. During the summer months, this is where the "action" is in terms of seeing a crowd of seals actually frolicking and moving about (at "haul-out" spots such as Kean Pt, the seals mostly just lay around, resting from a

night of swimming/hunting). At Ohau Point there'll be plenty of cute seal pups in the summertime, as well as all the drama that seal courtship entails—roaring bulls, tussling juveniles, squawking moms, territory battles, etc…all with seals surfing some waves also—quite a show! There are a variety of roadside pull-out spots with one signed boardwalk overlook site.

*Ohau Falls
seal pups*

Ohau Falls. 23km north of Kaikoura, 1km north of the signed seal colony viewpoint. If you've read this far you deserve a treat, and here it is. Ohau waterfall's little pool is just a 5-minute walk from the easy-to-miss turnout on SH1, just north of the main seal colony lookout stop. This waterfall may be NZ's most interesting waterfall, but only if you're lucky! A little-known nugget of info is that seal pups often make the difficult 300-ish meter rock-hop up to the waterfall simply to splash, swim, and play in the small waterfall pool. It seems that the seals may only go up to the waterfall pool in the autumn and winter, but nobody seems to know for sure. Personally, I haven't seen any pups-at-play the two summer visits that I've made to Ohau.

The pix here are from Brit travelers Jonty and Louise Abbott, who had this magic experience with the seal pups at the waterfall in June 2010. There had to be 12 or more pups playing in the pool when they arrived! No matter when you visit Kaikoura, pull off SH1 and make the easy walk—who knows? Even without seal pups you'll marvel how the pups would even know to clamber up the stream. Do their moms somehow tell them that there's a waterfall playpen up at the end?? Gotta Love NZ—an amazing sight around every corner!!

Watch the YouTube vids!!!

Amazing!!!

Louise and 12 new friends

A15 ▶ KAIKOURA
(kye-koora)

WHALE-WATCH CAPITAL OF NZ

Walk: various

• watch Meet the Locals: "Kaikoura"

OBSCUR-O-METER

The Kaikoura section of the South Island's eastern seaboard is one of the most dramatic coastlines in the country. The Seaward Kaikoura Mountains literally knife into the blue sea, especially when seen from Kaikoura or points south. The section of SH1 from 20km south of Kaikoura to 70km north is indisputably the finest coastal driving scenery in all of NZ—indisputably! On a sunny afternoon it'll blow you away!

Kaikoura itself is seeing a renaissance as a tourism mecca based on its abundant sea life viewing opportunities. Most of the action is whale/dolphin watching and it happens far offshore—so expect to pay for a tour to have any chance of seeing a whale—they don't swim close to shore at all. The SealSwim program is also said to be fabulous (I haven't done it in Kaikoura, but when I swam with seals in Mexico, the experience was amazing!) Also around Kaikoura is an abundance of NZ Fur seals. In Kaikoura and along SH1 the seals are everywhere (as opposed to the West Coast's general seal scarcity) (see Seal info, App. 3).

Unlike some other touristy get-on-the-water towns, namely the North's Paihia, Kaikoura has plenty to occupy you when you're not on a paid tour. There are the famed Fur seal colonies to view, coastal/headland walking tracks, inland viewpoint tracks, good surf beaches…and everything comes with the smashing view! Kaikoura is worth the trip on any NZ itinerary.

Pt. Kean seal colony. Everyone's must-see—expect tourist hordes all clustered around can't-be-bothered seals who have hauled-out onto the

View from Kaikoura Peninsula Track

Seaward Kaikoura Mtns.

Kaikoura

8 tourists and one seal at Point Kean

rocks to sun and rest. This is a haul-out site for seals, so they don't do much here except lay there. To see more active seals, head to the Ohau Point breeding colony.

Kaikoura Peninsula Walkway. The town's most popular walk. It begins at either Pt Kean or at the less-busy South Bay. The i-Site encourages a 3-hour loop made from town, but this involves a dullish 1.5 hours of roadside walking. If you have a car just drive to Pt Kean and do an out/back or a shoreline/ridgetop loop. The shoreline portion is low-tide only. If you don't want to walk the entire way from Pt Kean to South Bay you can shorten the loop by using the Whaler's Bay midpoint shortcut. There are mapboards at each carpark detailing the route.

South Bay Maori sculptures

Kiwa Road surf beaches. 12km north of Kaikoura on SH1. Turn onto Kiwa Rd just 2km north of the Hapuku Bridge. This gravel road cruises by 1.5 km of beachside parking spots and surf breaks. The most surfing action is often at the "Meatworks" break down near the road-end.

Iron Gate Stream swimming hole. 17km north of Kaikoura on SH1. At the signed bridge for Iron Gate Stream, park on the seaward shoulder and look for the faint path that heads upstream about 125m to a swimming hole. The stream doesn't look like much from the road, but the pool and its sunny little waterslide cascade hide just around the first bend of the stream.

Great afternoon sun for a tan and refreshing freshwater rinse. Wear sandals and bring a cold one (cans!).

A16 ▶ HAUMURI BLUFFS ROUTE
(how-murry)

A COASTAL ADVENTURE TRAMP

Walk: easy/difficult 6 km one-way beach scramble

• bring: shoes/water sandals, camera, loud voice, TIDE CHART

OBSCURE   POPULAR

OBSCUR-O-METER

DRIVING: 20km south of Kaikoura. Park on the north side of the Oaro railroad overbridge along the beach. Coming from the south this is where SH1 emerges onto the coast after the super-twisty inland bit.

The low-tide walk from Oaro to the Haumuri Bluffs is one of the strangest outings described in this book. The destination was an arch called "Spy Glass Point" out at the seaward tip of the Haumuri Bluffs. Alas, the arch caved-in in 2007, thus lessening the allure of rambling all the way to the point…but still leaving a VERY interesting off-the-beaten-track excursion. The route is this: at the point where SH 1 veers inland from the coast, you park and begin walking south next to the railroad tracks (which continue along the shore). The first 50-ish minutes of the route (4km) follows the RR tracks until they head into a tunnel under the bluffs. At this point you then scramble down to the shoreline and rock-hop for another 40 minutes (1.5km) until you reach the former arch (now a slot-tunnel) where you can scramble up the grassy bluff-top for a great view back over the Kaikoura Coast and the Seaward Mtns.

The neat thing about this route is all the special places along the way. The first is just 5 minutes from the last of the beach cottages. Directly under the tall white-ish limestone cliffs, if you peer down on the RR embankment you'll see 200m of scattered remains of a train wreck that the sea has been attempting to reclaim for years. The rusting wheels and rail cars are quite fascinating—where else can you see a seaweed-

Spy Glass Point   Fossils   Tunnel   Mikonui Beach

encrusted train wreck?? From there it's another 15 minutes to Mikonui Beach—a long stretch of welcoming sands and waves begging a splash (you can walk the beach and regain the RR tracks, but it requires a brushy-rocky scramble at the south end.) From Mikonui Beach it is another 30 minutes along the RR track's road to the tunnel.

Train wreck ruins

At the tunnel this route becomes much more difficult…and frought with HAZARDS! First off, the rock-hop route along the coves to the point is LOW-TIDE ONLY. If you don't know what the tide is doing, then you don't belong down in these coves—getting caught by a rising tide here could be very dangerous! So, after finding the steep scramble-path down to the shoreline, the real adventure begins. Here are the HAZARDS: Fur Seals!! Lots of them!! At low tide it seems that this stretch of coast now hosts a large number of scary seals sunning and basking on the rocks…and WHOA, they are difficult to see amongst the rocks until you are almost upon them and they ROAR in surprise!! These are no human-adjusted seals like at Kaikoura's Kean Pt—NO WAY…these are large wild mammals unaccustomed to being startled by humans walking on their beach. You'll be ambling along, your eyes cast down paying attention to the rock-hopping when ROOOAAAAR, you'll surprise a seal who is nestled in the shade of a rock you are about to hop—YIKES!!! Believe me, as the seal snarls and

41

cont'd ▶

hustles in fright towards the sea, your adrenalin will spike (after about 3 of these frightening surprises, scaring the wits outta me, I learned to clap and shout ahead as well as tossing stones to alert any lounging seals of my approach. Believe me, if you are frightened of snarling seals, then skip this rock-hop to the point! On the other hand, if you actually came to NZ for a bit of adventure—not the Kiwi-manufactured kind—then on to the point you go, staying as high as you can such that the startled seals can avoid you by scrambling towards the sea.

Fossil Rocks

The 40-ish minute rock-hop along the coves features some really interesting rock formations. Just a few minutes into the coves look for the rocks festooned with fossils. At the half-way point notice some Moeraki-type sand-stone concretion boulders being "birthed" from the sandstone walls. At the final point you'll see limestone layer-caking, and if you shoo the seals away from the passage so you can go through to the south side, where you'll (possibly) find some dangling ropes that can assist a climb to the top of the bluffs. The "pinch-point" for a rising tide is just before the point, so once you head back and get around the point, the rest of the journey back will be "all clear".

Seaward Kaikouras
Kaikoura
Haumuri Bluff Viewpoint

Hike ▶ This route should only be done on a falling tide! The tidal "pinch points" are in the final 10 minutes, thus about 2 hours from the start. So, if you begin just past high tide, then when you get to Te Pupaki Point, the tide will be low enough to pass, yet give you plenty of time to relax on the bluffs without worrying about getting pinched off on the way back.

After parking on the SH 1 shoulder, walk along the beach heading south with a hop over the Oaro stream (if stream is high then take the railbridge over it). At the end of the beach climb up to the RR track's road. The route now follows this RR roadway for the next 4km. In 5 minutes look for the wreck. In 20 minutes is Mikonui Beach. At 50-ish minutes comes the RR tunnel—you need to go past the tunnel entrance on the left for 40 meters to find the rough path angling steeply down to the beach—it's a bit overgrown and the last steps are difficult! Once on the "beach" the way to the point is simple, yet difficult—it's rock-hopping the entire way, shouting away the seals as you go. Be LOUD, have fun!

Spy Glass Point

Former Arch

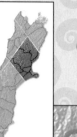

Christchurch and Passes

B

MAPS ON FLICKR!!!

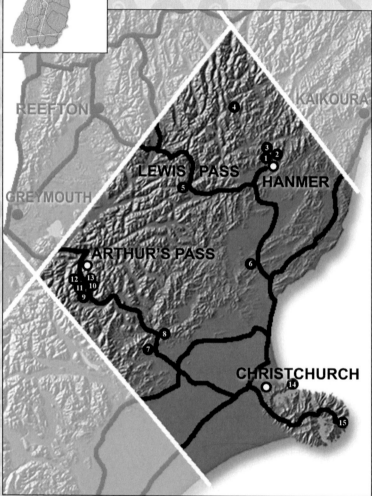

KAIKOURA

REEFTON

4

3
1 2

LEWIS PASS

HANMER

5

GREYMOUTH

ARTHUR'S PASS

12 13
11 10
9

6

8

7

CHRISTCHURCH

14

15

CHRISTCHURCH & PASSES

This section of the South Island hosts Christchurch, the South Island's biggest and most cosmopolitan city, as well as the two main highway arteries which cross the two passes, Arthur's and Lewis, to get to/from Christchurch. Christchurch (oft-abbreviated to "Chch") is often described as "more British than the Brits," meaning that it's a very "proper" city. Chch doesn't have all too much to WOW travelers—there are no must-see attractions like Wellington's Te Papa Museum or Auckland's Sky Tower/beaches/skyline. Of course you'll find sights, restaurants, bars, etc around the spacious central plaza, but don't expect architectural wonders or riveting history. Chch is a great city to live and work in, but not too fascinating to visit for long.

However, the two Southern Alps highways leading to/from Chch are very worth some in-depth exploring.

Arthur's Pass:

Arthur's Pass (920m) on SH 73 is the island's showcase high alpine driving route. This pass is impressive! Approaching Arthur's Pass from either direction you'll be treated to scenic winding valleys full of rushing blue-water rivers guiding you towards a skyline of snow-capped peaks. The premium "stop the car" mountain scenery is a 15km stretch around Arthur's Pass Village. This Village is an actual village, and therein lies its charm. It's just one shop/café, one restaurant/pub, some lodging, and a DOC Visitor Center…a nice small alpine village which hasn't been tarted-up. There are no tours or jet boats or bungys or gondolas—Arthur's Pass is simply nature's grandeur without any tourism hustle. Waterfalls spill from high, rocky crags scrape the skies, and mountaintop snowfields cap the visual glories. Arthur's Pass is a must-see for any South Island traveler!

Lewis Pass:

Lewis Pass (912m) on SH 7 is the lower-elevation "hot springs pass" between Westport and Chch. Lewis is the faster route through the mountains to/from Chch. Hanmer Springs is the uber-popular hot springs stop, but there's also the more serene Maruia Springs Resort and the free 'n' natural (yet troublesome) Sylvia Flats hot pools. Lewis Pass features some minor walks and waterfalls, but nothing much to compare to Arthur's grandeur and walking tracks.

Don't Miss:
Arthur's Pass
Devil's Punchbowl Falls (10)
Hanmer backroads (1-3)
Cave Stream (8)

B1 ▶ HANMER SPRINGS

FAMED HOT SPRING RESORT TOWN

Walk: various
- FYI: the Hanmer library has free unlimited Wifi
- Watch YouTube: zmfd-gwt2ug

OBSCUR-O-METER

Hanmer's main draw is its "Alpine Thermal Resort." In summertime the "alpine" is a bit of a stretch, given that Hanmer is at a snowless 300 meters of elevation, but regardless, people love the place and you should expect a busy summertime tourist crowd. In wintertime snow drapes all the nearby peaks, making for some great "alpine" vistas from the hot pools.

The thermal resort isn't all there is to Hanmer. Within the town there's a forest park laced with walking tracks, there's a tramp-able 1,300m Mt Isobel backing the town, and there are some great back-road driving tours that get you off the beaten path and into some sweet remote landscapes. Thus, come to Hanmer for the famed hot water springs, but leave time to explore the lesser-known free natural attractions.

Hanmer Alpine Thermal Resort.

This place is fun to visit! Prepare your expectations though, as there's nothing natural about the artificially crafted pools lined with both real and fake rocks. Hanmer is more of a busy people-watching place than a quiet meditative spot. That's the fun of Hanmer's springs —the summertime crowd of

Hanmer Pools

international visitors who hop from pool to pool to find one "just right" for the moment. The resort has about a dozen different pools of different sizes and temperatures. Everyone seems to constantly hop from one pool to the next, providing an interesting palette of international swimsuit styles, body types, and flirting habits. It's like a big beach party every day, rain or shine. It costs roughly $15 per person to use the pools.

Dog Stream Falls

Dog Stream Waterfall track.
Check the i-Site for the Hanmer Forest Tracks map. This track is a steep 45 minutes to the falls, with many stairways towards the end. The falls are 40m high and very narrow. Bring sandals so you can stand in the small rocky waterfall pool for a shower on a hot day. The route was the Hanmer Forest's best loop track, but logging has closed the "down" side of the loop as of 2010— check with the i-Site for info whether the loop portion has re-opened.

From downtown Hanmer take Jollies Pass Rd for 2km then turn left onto McIntyre for 3km unsealed to carpark.

B2 ▶ JOLLIES PASS/JACK'S PASS DRIVING LOOP ROUTE

FABULOUSLY SCENIC GRAVEL LOOP DRIVE ABOVE HANMER

Drive: 26km of 2WD gravel roads

● bring: Hanmer town map

OBSCUR-O-METER

This loop drive is a fabulous gravel road route that takes you from Hanmer up and over one pass, down to the pretty Clarence River canyon north of Hanmer's Mtns, then back up and over the other pass to complete a loop back to town. This route (or a portion of it) is a must-do for anyone wanting to appreciate Hanmer for more than just its commercialized charms. The entire driving route is about 26km total from Hanmer and would take about 45 minutes if you drove it non-stop. But stop you will because the views and scenery are fantastic! The Jollies Pass viewpoint is almost like being atop Mt Isobel, but without the tramping effort! Any 2WD car is OK, but oversize or larger campervans/RVs may want to skip the steeper-narrower Jollies Pass side (and only go out/back up Jack's and down to Clarence River).

The best route for normal cars/vans is going counter-clockwise. From Hanmer head up Jollies Pass Rd, setting your odometer in town. In 4km you'll arrive at the former site of Jollies' hotel and begin the gravel portion of the route. Up you go for a slow 3.6km more to reach the "Jollies Pass" sign (7.6km). (Detour left here on the powerlines-access road for a short 300m detour to an exceptional view under the powerlines.) Retreating

Along Clarence River

back to the Jollies sign go left and descend to the Clarence River (12km mark). Go left for 6km along the river (upstream) then left again at the next junction to climb to Jack's Pass (21 km) and then over the pass finish the route back to town (26km.)

B3 ▶ MT. ISOBEL TRACK

THE MTN TOP OVERLOOKING HANMER SPRINGS

Tramp: Strenuous 70-min (4km) one-way

- Elevation Jack's Pass carpark: 860m
- Elevation Mt. Isobel Trig: 1362m

OBSCURE POPULAR
OBSCUR-O-METER

The Mt Isobel Track starts at Jack's Pass above Hanmer and climbs steeply to Isobel's 1,362m viewpoint Trig. This is the most easily-accessed strenuous track in the Hanmer area, and after summiting Mt Isobel you'll have more than earned a nice relaxing soak in the hot pools.

Mt. Isobel Trig

Hanmer Springs

The tramping route is a fairly relentless 60-70 minutes up for fit trampers (4km). Be prepared for some loose and super-steep sections. Widely-spaced poles mark the route, but for the most part just keep climbing until you can't climb any-more. Strangely, when you're 2/3 the way up a DOC sign says that the peak is an hour more, but it isn't—it's only 20-25 more minutes from there. At the top you'll get superb views of the entire Hanmer Valley and over the southern ridge to the Waiau River Valley. Looking north you'll see down into the scenic Clarence River canyon which flows from here all the way north of Kaikoura, where it dumps into the sea at Clarence.

Clarence River Valley

DRIVING: From Hanmer Springs follow the road signs towards Jack's Pass and then take Jack's Pass Rd for 7km of winding gravel up to the carpark at top of the pass.

B4 ▶ LAKE TENNYSON

PRISTINE OFF-THE-BEATEN TRACK LAKESIDE CAMPING SPOT

Drive: 40km of washboardy gravel road from Hanmer to lake

● elevation lake: 1080m

OBSCUR-O-METER

Want to camp next to a sapphire blue alpine lake with drive-up access and have almost guaranteed solitude? Lake Tennyson delivers! This lake lies far far far off the beaten track, hidden on the sunny side of the Southern Alps and glimmering under a ridge of snow-capped peaks. Lake Tennyson is a rough hour-long 2WD-drive from Hanmer if you're willing to drive fast on washboardy gravel road. If you're not willing to "haul-ass" on bad gravel washboard, then skip Lake Tennyson as the road would be torturously slow and wearying for a less-aggressive driver.

Lake Tennyson

Arriving finally at Lake Tennyson, chances are good you'll be the only ones there. Just you, the lake, the mountains, a free camp area and a long-drop toilet. No homes, no tracks, no dock, no nothing…just unspoiled NZ wilderness. The lake is the headwaters of the Clarence River—the river you drive beside for 32km…which flows all the way to north of Kaikoura. Lake Tennyson is the super-rare NZ lake which has drive-up access, yet no development whatsoever. Come prepared because Lake Tennyson is the proverbial "far-from-it-all"—there's virtually no sign of civilization between Hanmer and the lake. Be SURE you have a spare tire! Be sure you have enough beer!

(Personally, I've only gone to Tennyson once, for a day trip. Once there I kicked myself for not having got supplies to spend the night (beer!). I had NO IDEA how beautiful and unspoiled the lake would be. I suggest going for the night if you're going to go at all!!)

DRIVING: 2WD OK. From Hanmer head 9km over Jack's Pass and down to the Clarence River. Turn left and follow the unsealed 32km to the signed left turn to the lake. (It takes about 45 minutes for the washboardy 32km if you drive FAST!)

B5 ▶ SYLVIA FLATS HOT SPRING
SOUTH ISLAND'S MOST ACCESSIBLE NATURAL HOT SPRING POOL

Walk: easy 100m

- No long drop as of 2010
- Bring: DEET, swimsuit (for the rocky bottom on your bottom), cans, NO GLASS

OBSCUR-O-METER

Devil by daylight, nectar by night! The Sylvia Flats small riverside hot pools, just a 100m walk from a roadside picnic stop on the Lewis Pass Hwy (SH7), would be wonderful…except they're NOT! Some quirk of pure evil plagues these pools with the most awful swarm of sandflies EVER! Honestly, you've not seen a sandfly swarm until you've seen this one…stop and take a look, but BE WARNED!

But, that said, the "nectar by night" phrase is true. The sandflies go to bed after dark, leaving just you, the rush of the river, and the Southern Cross for a relaxing soak in the 40° waters. There are basically one or two volunteer-dug pools an arm's length from the Lewis River. There are no restrictions on overnight parking…so come after dark, have a soak and then leave. Don't camp here—it's not worth it…these little reverse-vampires arise with the dawn to plague you anew before you can even put your billy to boil. Yikes! Sadly, there will be no enjoyable morning soak at Sylvia – the plague will be waiting once you step outside for a morning leak. You've been warned.

For a much better place to camp head north on SH7 for 10.5km to DOC's Deer Valley free camp along the same Lewis River. There are nice riverside sites and a long-drop…and fire wood seems abundant for the fire pit that exists at each site. And, lo and behold, much fewer sandflies! Set up camp here, head to the pools after dark for a soak, and then come back for a sleep knowing that you "did" Lewis Pass the smart way.

2 riverside hot pools

50

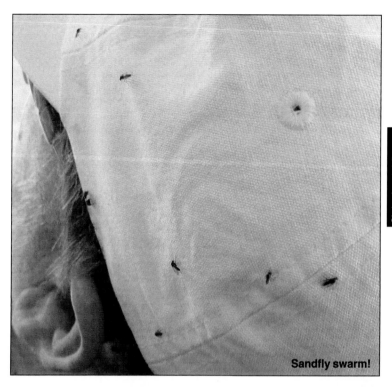

Sandfly swarm!

For a bit of exercise, 2.7km east of Sylvia Flats is one end of the St James Walkway. The sandflies aren't too bad here and for an easy walk you can go up the track 30 minutes to an old-time wire-only swingbridge across the creek.

DRIVING: The hot spring carpark is only signed with a typical blue highway "picnic" sign—no mention of the hot pools or any other wording. On SH 7, from the west the Sylvia Flats "picnic stop" is only marked by a blue "400m ahead" sign. It's 20km south of Maruia Hot Springs, 10.5km past Deer Valley DOC camp.

From the east on SH 7 it's 50 km from Hanmer's junction, 2.7 km past the signed St James track/Boyle River.

B6 ► WAIKARI MAORI ROCK ART SITE

A STEEP WALK TO A MAORI ROCK ART SITE

Walk: Steep moderate 40-minute one-way (about 2.5 km)

● watch YouTube: ziviph4b_os

Christchurch & Passes

The Waikari Maori rock art site is one of the South Island's finest examples of ancient rock art on public land. The drawings here are on a 25m section of a limestone overhang, protected with typical NZ rock art fencing. The drawings were done with charcoal and red ochre. Anthropologists theorize that the Maoris used this overhang as a camp spot while hunting in the once-abundant forest that covered the area...possibly on a route between coast and mountains.

The first Pakeha (white man) scientific study of the rock art was commissioned in 1876 and found evidence of stone tools and campsite remains. Over the next 50 years scientists visited the site to copy the drawings until puzzlingly, in 1929, the Dominion Museum director had his investigators over-paint some of the drawings with black and red house paint to make them better visible. Incredible defacement in the name of science!

Thus, nowadays you'll see a background of very faint charcoal drawings and an array of very distinct house paint mock-ups. The art is still very interesting, regardless of the over-paint. The

dinosaur-eating-the-man is especially peculiar …wasn't the Moa the biggest animal around back then? Curious too are the dated graffiti signatures from 100+ years back that occupy much of the space between drawings. Seems that W. Johnston may win the prize for the first to deface the site…but you decide.

Walk Walk uphill on SH7 50m to find the signed track and route map (across from Weka Pass railway). The track follows the former railbed about 700m to a signed stile where you'll turn left and begin ascending the hillside following the fenceline and marker poles. It's a steep 1km climb, taking about 25 minutes up the hill, but at least you've got great Southern Alps views when you stop to catch your breath. Then comes a 10-minute 500m descent down the backside to the long limestone outcrop that awaits down and to the right. Overall this outing will probably take 1.5 to 2 hours.

DRIVING: The township of Waikari is on SH7, 50km south of Hanmer or 14km north of Waipara. To find the track park along SH 7 on the south side of the commercial strip near the *G.A.S. station* and *Star & Garter Pub*. The track begins at a sign along SH 7.

B7 ▷ CASTLE HILL

PHANTASMAGORIC NARNIA ROCKSCAPE

**Walk: easy/moderate 3-5 km rambling
exploratory routes**
- elevation carpark: 750m
- elevation Castle Hill Trig: 920m

OBSCUR-O-METER

Castle Hill is a ridge of limestone boulders rising directly above SH 73 in the eastern foothills of the Southern Alps. The area is basically a fun maze of fabulously odd eroded grey limestone outcroppings. There are no marked tracks—the fun is weaving into and over the boulders, creating your own adventure. Walking amongst these bizarre shapes you can't help but think "Lord of the Rings"…but nope, it's Narnia! This landscape is so surreal you'd think it a Weta Studios CGI creation, but instead you'll have to check the end of "The Lion, the Witch, and the Wardrobe" to see the climactic Castle Hill battle scenes filmed near here in 2004.

These eye-popping boulders have been a tourist stop since the 1800s, but until DOC opened a carpark and added signage in 2004, these rocks were largely just a rock-climber's playground. There's an entire book detailing the Castle Hill climbing routes, including the story of when the world's best rock climber, Chris Sharma, paid a visit to Castle Hill to test himself against the hardest local routes. (For Sharma footage, check YouTube kssqg5uy and pa-kngeu9bi.)

Castle Hill Loop Route

Trig

Often travelers just make a quick photo-stop at Castle Hill, but if you're up for a little more than that, then you can make a sort of 5km-ish loop hike. Castle Hill itself is the highpoint atop the ridge in back of the western blob of rock (about 150m above the carpark). If you head between the two front-and-center outcroppings and then skirt the

protected area, you then can work your way up to Castle Hill's Trig and the prominent 25m hill-top boulder. Great 360° views await at the top. From there head east along the ridge and back down the gully for a good overall Castle Hill tour.

DRIVING: From the west on SH73 the signed DOC Kura Tawhiti/ Castle Hill carpark is 7km south of Cave Stream, 4km south of Castle Hill Village.

From the east the carpark is 8km west of Lake Lyndon, about 80km from Christchurch.

B8 ▷ CAVE STREAM

AN EASILY EXPLORABLE STREAM RUNNING THROUGH A CAVE

Tramp: moderate 1-hour wade/splash

- watch YouTube: kcLkcL--gy8
- bring: headlamps, warm get-wet clothing, sturdy get-wet shoes, two lights w/neck cords

OBSCURE POPULAR
OBSCUR-0-METER

Cave Stream is free NZ adventure as its finest...but sadly an adventure that most travelers miss out on because it's not promoted very well by DOC and travelers show up unprepared. Don't miss out... READ ON! Cave stream is a

Cave Stream entrance

fabulous all-ages adventure! Don your water shoes, shorts or pants to get wet in, maybe a long-sleeve top and hat if you're the chilly sort, and a head lamp and additional torch....then off you go into the circular cave opening for a 30-45 minute splashing underground jaunt through the amazing

Knee-deep in Cave Stream

limestone bowels of our fun-loving earth! Oh yeah, you'll get wet—mostly just knee-deep, but the first pool in the cave will gauge your shrinkage reaction with a crotch-deep section. This is an adventure...it's rugged and sometimes uncertain footing, it's DARK, it's chilly...and it is way-memorable fun!! (I've seen both kids and grandmas do it...Go for it!)

Most travelers show up a bit unprepared, as DOC does a lousy time preparing you ahead of time. That's what this book is for—to help you prepare so that you can make the best adventure out of your travels! Arriving at the Cave Stream carpark you'll be greeted with a DOC sign advising you to wear heaps, string the torch on your neck...and beware! This is all solid info, but DOC has to advise as if you may arrive there any time of the year. In summertime this cave adventure isn't nearly as dire as the signs may suggest. Still though, beware that big local rains will swell this stream into scary proportions. If the first pool is crotch-deep, then all is well and you'll be fine, even in shorts and a t-shirt. If it's been raining and brown unclear water is surging from the cave opening, then duh, don't go in!!

Cave exit ladder

Headlamps are best because you'll be climbing a bit and always using your hands to steady yourself against the walls. At the start of the cave you'll think your dim headlamp won't be enough, but once your eyes adjust after 3 minutes... you'll be fine. Flash photos work great inside the cave, so go ahead and bring your small camera in a backpack (maybe wrap it in a plastic bag).

Tramp Walk downhill to the downstream cave opening (it's best to go upstream within the cave). On with the lights and in you go! At the very end there is a deepish pool then a series of metal rungs to climb out of the pool and above the waterfall that ends the adventure. Atop the rungs you'll then crawl under an overhang and back out into the light.

Happy cavers

DRIVING: Cave stream is a well-signed carpark on SH 73 about 50km east of Arthur's Pass. Coming from the west go 14.4km past Lake Pearson (or 5.6km past Craigieburn Rec. Area).
    Coming from the east the signed carpark is 3km north of Castle Hill Village.

B9 ▶ HALPINS CREEK FALLS

ARTHUR'S PASS UNSUNG BIG WATERFALL

Tramp: difficult 20-minute streambed rock-hop

● bring: water shoes, bathing suit

OBSCUR-O-METER

Rock-hop route

Of all the big waterfalls of Arthur's Pass, guess which is my favorite? Right…the one with no publicity, no signs, no track…and no tourists. Halpins Creek Falls only shows a wee bit of its very top from the highway—if you want to see it all you've got to go up the stream-bed. You won't find any mention of this waterfall in the Visitor Center or anywhere else. The streambed route leading up to this giant waterfall is a fun challenge involving much rock-hopping and mini-waterfall climbing. Water shoes/sandals are a must, as you'll often be ankle-to-knee deep in the creek. The route is a challenge, but no more so than any bit of the Avalanche Peak tramp. If you're athletic and adventurous, you'll love Halpins Creek Falls!

The waterfall is about 70m high and on a sunny day, when you make it to the very base of the falls, the cooling mist will surround you with your own personal rainbow. This is a real-deal off-the-beaten-track New Zealand ahhhh! Often, if Arthur's pass is clouded in from the west, this waterfall may still be sunny, or at least less rainy. And, another bonus of the entire excursion is that in early summer you get to park amidst a huge meadow of blue Lupine wildflowers—a great place to begin and end a fun adventure!

Tramp ▶ Walk down into the creekbed by the rail tracks—you'll see the very top of the falls from here. Now just head up the creekbed, crossing back and forth numerous times.

DRIVING: On SH 73, Halpins Creek is 4km east of Arthur's Pass Village or 2km west of roadside Greyney's Shelter. To access the creek bed you'll need to turn down the gravel road (along the Rail tracks) about 400m west of the creek. Coming from Arthur's Village it's easy to miss this unsigned turn, but just go 2km then turn around and come back once you know where the creek is.

Christchurch & Passes

B10 DEVIL'S PUNCHBOWL FALLS
SOUTH ISLAND'S BEST WATERFALL OUTSIDE OF FIORDLAND

Walk: moderate 15-minute 1.0 km track
- watch YouTube: eqoiu_fLec4
- elevation carpark: 750m
- elevation viewpoint: 820m

OBSCUR-O-METER
OBSCURE — POPULAR

131m!

Devil's Punchbowl Falls is the must-see attraction of Arthur's Pass. This waterfall is as near to perfect as you can ask for—high, mighty, and mesmerizing with numerous view vantages. High above Arthur's Pass Village the creek spits from a notch in the rocky ridge and cascades 131 meters in ethereal splendor. The waterfall gets great afternoon light, making it quite transfixing to simply sit on the view platform and study the myriad of feathery wisps.

A quick track heads from the signed carpark 500m west of the village center (or just walk from the village.) The track is only about 1km, but it's mostly steps and stairways—you've got to earn your up-close date with this Devil! At the view platform a constant misty spray will tickle your skin and spot-up your photo attempts (bring a lens cloth).

Other than just gaping at the falls, there's a rough slippery path up from the platform that accesses the wind-whipped waterfall pool. Amazingly enough some people go for a quick dip in this devilishly cold pool....brrrrrr, talk about "cold as hell"!

Punchbowl swimmers...brrrr

59

B11 ► AVALANCHE PEAK LOOP TRAMP

SOUTH ANSWER TO THE TONGARIRO CROSSING (TOUGHEST DAY–HIKE ON THE ISLAND)

Tramp: Difficult 5-hour loop (10km)

● elev top: 1800m ● elev Arthur's Pass: 700m
● watch YouTube: fetrunt7wn8
● bring: warm clothing, weather forecast

OBSCUR-O-METER

The Avalanche Peak loop track is arguably the finest day walk/tramp on the South Island. It's <u>Definitely</u> the best alpine day-<u>loop</u> on the Island! It is also VERY difficult and fatiguing, completely different than the mostly-easy "Great Walks". Your legs will probably be sore for days after this tramp!

Combining the Scotts Track and the Avalanche Peak Track for a loop starting/finishing at Arthur's Pass Village, you'll ascend 1,100 vertical meters to the summit and its jaw-dropping 360° views. The magnificent views at the peak (and on the way up) encompass hanging glaciers, barren craggy peaks, cascading waterfalls…and often a flock of Keas begging handouts. The route, as every DOC publication will tell you, is a <u>fine-weather-only</u> route. The weather can get brutally cold and windy above the bush line and change from fair to awful in minutes. Don't attempt this track in blustery changeable weather—what's the sense of tramping to a viewpoint peak when everything is clouded-in and there's no views? Any i-Site on the island can call up to DOC's Arthur's office to get a local forecast—make sure you do. The weather on the West Coast may be grey and low clouds, but the weather up at Arthur's may be brilliant sun the same day…thus, call ahead and find out. By way of comparison to the North Island's famed Tongariro Crossing, the Avalanche Peak loop tramp is shorter, but more difficult, than the Tongariro—as there's not one flat spot on the entire Avalanche loop.

Avalanche Peak seen from Temple Basin

Avalanche Peak Track

Bealey Valley

Scotts Track

Arthur's

Here's an opinion on which direction to take: The VisCtr seems to direct people up Avalanche and down Scotts. I personally think that's backwards. I say go up Scotts. Here's why... Scotts track has all

Arthur's Village

On the Scotts Track

the views the entire way up—way more than Avalanche. Since the route is SO fricking steep, you'll have to stop and rest plenty, so taking pix on the way up will be fun as each step delivers a better view of Punchbowl/Bridal Veil falls and Mt Rolleston. Thus, on Scotts Track rest stops become photo

Kea at the peak

stops, much more so than on the Avalanche Peak Track where the views on the way up are limited. Also, what if the clouds come in when you're half way up and shut down all the views? Well, climbing Scotts at least you've had good views and photos on the way up in case you decide to turn back. And thirdly, either route is so super-steep and rugged that coming down you'll have little opportunity to look around—you'll be watching each foot-step... and be tired and more reluctant to whip out the camera anyhow. Once you've been to the peak, the descending views on Scotts will not impress as much as they do on the way up. 'Nuff said...I say to ascend the view track—Scotts—and then trudge the descent down Avalanche track.

Tramp ▶ Park in the Devil's Punchbowl carpark. Walk out to SH 73 and go uphill along the roadside for 250m, cross the bridge and find the signed Scotts Track on the left. The grueling climb begins immediately and never lets up for about 2.5 hours to the peak. The Avalanche Peak track joins in from the left about 5 minutes below the top, signaled by the

marker poles becoming doubled. The Avalanche route descends the obvious ridgeline angling down towards Arthur's Village, steep from the junction. The descent will take about 2 hours, with the final 300-ish meters enlivened by the numerous cascades of Avalanche Creek Falls.

Avalanche Peak

B12 ▶ BEALEY VALLEY TRACK

RUGGED ROUTE UP A GLACIER-CHOKED CANYON

**Tramp: difficult one-hour one-way
(about 300m elevation gain in 2.5km)**
- elevation carpark: 780m
- elevation snowfield: 1080m

OBSCUR-O-METER

The Bealey Valley Track is a rugged tramp—don't be fooled by the "valley" in the name—this is more a rocky avalanche canyon than a *Sound of Music* valley. The track is a one-hour roots 'n' rock-hop up the Bealey Stream to the snow-choked canyon at its head. Besides the majestic towering valley walls and waterfalls, the most interesting feature of Bealey Valley is the vast perennial snowfield that blocks-up the upstream end of the valley. This snowfield is a "false glacier", meaning that it is avalanche snow that gets packed and squeezed so deep into the bottom of the valley that it begins to act as a flowing glacier. The route up the streambed leads straight into the gaping, dripping, waterfall-gushing maw of this icy marvel. The cave-mouth of this false glacier is wet, slippery, cold…and prone to rocks falling from its ceiling that have been avalanched down with the snow—it's probably best not to venture in.

But, since it seems somewhat unsatisfying to end this adventure at the glacial snout with its limited views, backtrack a bit and clamber up the left slope for a steep 10 minute scramble to gain a satisfyingly WoW perch overlooking both the glacier and the 60m waterfalls pouring into it. From these higher perches above the glacier you can also see northwards to the entire Temple Basin Ski Area and wispy Twin Creek Falls.

Heading up Bealey Valley

FYI ▶ Temple Basin is a peculiar ski area in that you can't drive up its too-steep access road—you have to walk! In the winter a lift carries your equipment up, but you have to walk up the roadway slope to access the ski area's lifts. Whew, hard core Kiwi!

Snowfield

View from above final snowfield

Tramp ▶ Begin up the signed track as it zigzags up through the forest for 30 minutes. You'll emerge into the streambed area where the markings stop...but simply continue up the stream's shoulder until ice blocks the way.

DRIVING: The Bealey Valley carpark is 2.7km NW from Arthur's Village, adjacent to Jack's Hut.

OTHER WATERFALLS OF ARTHUR'S VILLAGE

Walk: various walks

● bring: water sandals

OBSCUR-O-METER

(sidebar) Christchurch & Passes

Bridal Veil Falls. The track to Bridal Veil begins at the same bridge to Devil's Punchbowl. The track and the viewpoint of this waterfall are a bit disappointing. The track is a nice bush track and all, but it only delivers a wee peak at part of the distant Veil. After this glimpse the track then continues up and down before depositing you onto the highway…where you can walk the busy highway back to the carpark or just backtrack. What's the point?

The much better way to see Bridal Veil's true glory is to tramp up the Scotts Track for 20-30 minutes (towards Avalanche Peak). The beginning of this track gives you a postcard view of Devil's punchbowl and Arthur's Village…and if you keep climbing a little, then Bridal Veil's entire waterfall canyon comes into view. The hard-to-find Scotts Track is about 300m up SH 73 from the Devil's Punchbowl carpark, just 50m past the Wardens Creek bridge (see entry B11).

Upper Twin Falls

Twin Creek Falls. Twin Creek delicately falls above the Temple Basin Ski Area carpark (3.5km northwest of the Village). Twin Creek Falls is long and slender, more whisper than roar. For a good look head up the skifields road for a few minutes to get a decent photo without powerlines in the foreground. From this skifield road you'll also get the valley's best view of Avalanche Peak and its entire tramping route.

The best way to enjoy Twin Creek Falls though is not by taking a picture, but rather taking a dive! One of Arthur's sneaky secrets is that a quick wet rock-hop just 8-10 minutes up the streambed from the carpark delivers you to a delightful waterfall pool. This final fall

Diving into
Lower Twin Falls

of all Twin Creek's tiers is a mere 15m, but it cascades into a deep rock-rimmed pool that gets great 1-3pm sun. The pool is deep and warmish enough for a dive, and the surrounding rocks smooth and inviting enough for a bask. Simply wonderful and completely unknown to the masses at Punchbowl!

Avalanche Creek Falls. Avalanche Creek has a waterfall viewpoint platform just a 5-minute walk behind the Visitor Center. But this final waterfall is only the last in line of many individual drops. There must be at least 300m of waterfalls up this creek. To see more of them begin up the Avalanche Peak track. This track is very steep (like the entire tramp to the peak), but if you want some more falls, then up you go and out various side paths to view higher waterfalls in this steep gorge.

B14 ▶ TAYLOR'S MISTAKE/ GODLEY HEAD LOOP TRACK

VIEW-PACKED HEADLANDS TRACK

Walk: moderate 2-hour walking loop (9km)
- elevation Taylors: 0m
- elevation top: 150m
- bring: sunscreen, sunhat, binoculars

OBSCUR-O-METER

This moderate loop track tours the grassy open slopes of Godley Headlands beginning from the last bit of Chch's eastern suburbs—Taylor's Mistake beach. Most of the track is gentle and there are ocean views 100% of the time, making this walk a nice escape from the city. After a 40-minute easy walk along the north-facing hills, enjoying views past the Brighton Pier and up the coast, you'll make a quick ascent up to Summit Rd's road-end carpark. This is the site of the remains of the WWII gun emplacements and the barracks where over 700 soldiers were stationed in 1941-2. A good optional 30-minute loop heads out to the headlands' point to see some of the historic bunkers and such. To finish the loop back to Taylor's you'll take the marked track 50-minutes back along the Lyttleton Harbor headlands, thankfully skirting the Trig hill rather than climbing it, before heading downhill back to Taylor's Mistake.

There's no shade the entire route, so bring the sunscreen and hat. There are mapboards both at Taylor's beach and up at Summit Rd—the route you want is the red loop. Sometimes the walk is a bit confusing because it weaves in and out with a Mtn-bike track…but it's fairly easy to head downhill and end up at Taylor's Mistake.

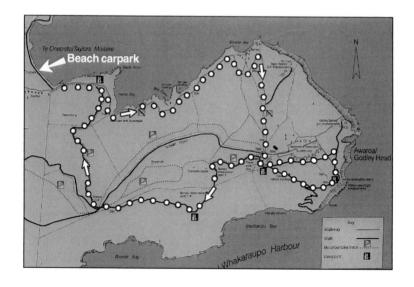

Historic army buildings

View to Banks Peninsula from gunnery emplacement

DRIVING: From downtown Chch it's about a 30-minute drive to Taylor's Mistake Beach. Head east towards Sumner and just past Sumner's beach, in the middle of the town, turn left onto Naylands Rd and follow it over to the hill then up the steep road and over/down to Taylor's Mistake beach carpark.

67

Christchurch & Passes

B15 ▶ HINEWAI'S "HIDDEN" HIKING

BANKS PENINSULA'S BEST PUBLIC WALKING/ TRAMPING TRACKS

Walk: difficult 3-4 hour loop, or shorter walks from the beach area
- Google: "DOC Hinewai"
- bring: swimsuit, Hinewai map

OBSCURE — POPULAR
OBSCUR-O-METER

The Hinewai Reserve is the Banks Peninsula's best hidden secret. The entire Banks Peninsula is almost entirely denuded pasture, except for small areas such as Hinewai…and Hinewai is by far the best bit of regenerating forest on the peninsula. The reason that the area is "hidden" is because the valley is a private land trust set aside for forest/ wildlife regeneration and visitation. "Hinewai" is the nickname of the area, and thus it doesn't appear on maps—look for the Otanerito Valley/Bay. Also, since DOC doesn't manage the site, it gets no mention in their literature…and since DOC doesn't mention it, it means none of the mainstream guidebooks mention it either…thus, "hidden" Hinewai.

Most mentions you hear of walking tracks on the peninsula mention the privately operated "Banks Peninsula" multi-day track. But guess what…you can walk the Hinewai bit of this track (the 4th day section) for FREE as a long day walk. An additional bonus of exploring Hinewai is that they've made an access arrangement with the Otanerito Bay homestead to walk through their lands to access their beach…and a great beach it is—sandy and welcoming rather than the peninsula's more common rocky/ shingled coves. Hinewai's walking loop encompasses a nice variety of forest types—some dense bush, some open views, some gurgling stream, some dry Gorse-scapes….basically a REALLY nice bush walk, with a great beach in the middle!

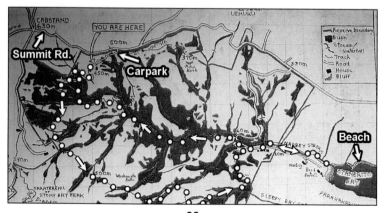

Arriving at Hinewai's hidden carpark you'll find a detailed hand-drawn map of the walking/tramping tracks... detailing the various lookouts/ water-falls/ big trees and such. This map is an introduction to the care that Hinewai receives

Otanerito Bay

View from "500m" vista

from its resident caretaker, Hugh Wilson. Hugh's dedication to Hinewai's conservation is evident on every step of the track, every informative sign at every junction. Hinewai is Hugh's Labor of Love—hopefully you'll meet him because he's both super-friendly and incredibly knowledgeable! Every visit should start with a stop at the Visitor Center just down from the carpark. You'll learn more about Gorse than you thought you'd ever want...as well as to get a look at 20 years of "forest-regenerating" photos of the valley—quite interesting!

Walk ▶ Hugh will tell you that the best walking circuit is the long 3-4 hour loop that traverses the far ridge down to the beach then comes back up the stream gully back to the VisCtr. This is the best track for an all-day outing, and the best way to do it is to plan for a half-way stop down at the beach for a picnic/swim/sun before the 60-80 minute streamside uphill back to the VisCtr. The elevation gain of the loop is only 530m, but all the up/down makes it feel like an 800m vertical outing. Thus, this is a difficult loop, not an easy day-hike.

Otanerito Bay

For an easier outing you could drive down the road all the way to the beach carpark and do an out/back up the Valley Track to Boundary Falls—this would be about 45-min one-way.

DRIVING: Hinewai is directly above Akaroa, off of Long Bay Rd, at the end of the "tourist" Summit Rd. From Akaroa, 2km before Akaroa, turn up the signed Long Bay Rd and climb 5km until the 5-way intersection with Summit Rd. To find Hinewai go straight here, towards "Goughs Bay" (look for the small Hinewai sign below "Goughs"). Go 1.5 km down this road to the signed Hinewai carpark on the right.

West Coast - NORTH

MAPS ON FLICKR!!!

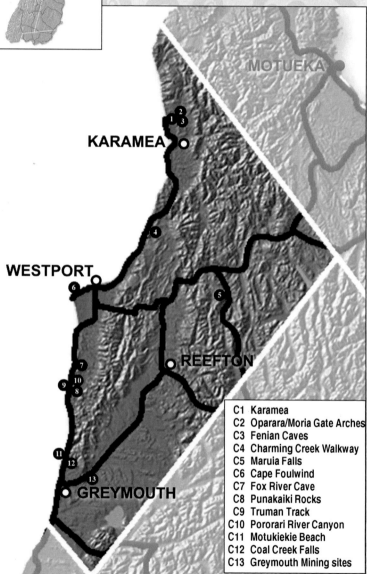

MOTUEKA

KARAMEA

WESTPORT

REEFTON

GREYMOUTH

ARTHUR'S PASS

C1 Karamea
C2 Oparara/Moria Gate Arches
C3 Fenian Caves
C4 Charming Creek Walkway
C5 Maruia Falls
C6 Cape Foulwind
C7 Fox River Cave
C8 Punakaiki Rocks
C9 Truman Track
C10 Pororari River Canyon
C11 Motukiekie Beach
C12 Coal Creek Falls
C13 Greymouth Mining sites

WEST COAST - NORTH

The northern half of the South Island's wet 'n wild West Coast features Westland's two major cities, Westport and Greymouth, and one must-must-must-see natural wonder—the Punakaiki Rocks. Also featured is most travelers' first introduction to Westland's two banes—rain and sandflies.

Neither Westport nor Greymouth has too much to offer travelers except gas, groceries, hotels, etc. Both are industrial-type port towns established to service the local coal-mining industries. Neither is very scenic nor interesting, but there is good hearty dark beer to be had in each.

The main draw of the northern West Coast is Paparoa Nat'l Park's famed Punakaiki Rocks. These rock formations are affectionately known as the "pancake rocks" because the rocks are stacked like pancakes and "pancake" is much easier for tourists to say and remember than Punakaiki. Regardless, these limestone rocks, perched directly above the sea and pocked with caves and crevices, put on one of NZ's finest natural shows when the waves are bashing at HIGH TIDE. The Pancake Rocks are on every tour-bus itinerary, but even having a gaggle of tourists around doesn't detract from the amazing spectacle when these rocks are rocking! You need/should/must plan ahead to visit Punakaiki at high tide, because this is when the blowholes explode with a ground-shaking earth-quaking rumble! At low tide nothing happens—it's just a bunch of funny-looking rocks barely worth a long look…but at high tide, whoa, LOOKOUT! Plan on a full day in the Punakaiki area, as there's plenty to see in Paparoa Nat'l Park while you wait for the high tide show (if the sea is calm, which is rare, then there's nothing to see…hurry on southwards).

For travelers who like to REALLY get off the beaten path, be sure to consider a trip north to Karamea. Karamea is worth the trip for folks not on a hurry-up itinerary. Karamea just feels different…you'll see.

Don't miss:
Punakaiki Rocks! (8)
Motukiekie Rocks shoreline (11)
Charming Creek Walkway (4)

THE POT OF GOLD AT THE END OF THE ROAD

GET OFF THE BEATEN TRACK!

- No videos—too far off the Beaten Track!

OBSCURE   POPULAR
OBSCUR-O-METER

Karamea might be the Last Best Place. The last place on the South Island with attractions worth seeing, but virtually no summertime tourists. Not that Karamea wants it this way…they want tourists, but have yet to figure out how to get them to take a 100km detour from the typical West Coast route. Like moths to a campervan ceiling light the tourists hurry south to see Punakaiki, Hokitika, and the glaciers…leaving Karamea all by its lonesome. Karamea is what the Catlins once was…a nice beautiful place without a mob of branded tourist campervans. The road to Karamea is a long out 'n' back, similar to the road to Milford Sound. But Milford, obviously, is Milford, and Karamea isn't. But whereas Milford is overrun with hoopla and hustle, Karamea isn't. Karamea is one of the few visit-worthy South Island spots without a stack of commercial brochures, without a legion of $$ "adventures," without a dependable petrol supply, and without "No Overnight Staying" signs plastered on every road-end. Someday it'll probably have these, but not yet.

If you are on a hurry-hurry South Island tour, then skip Karamea. But if you have some time and enjoy getting "off-the-path", then plan a low-key couple of days in Karamea—you'll be delighted. Visit the arches, visit Heaphy's beaches, maybe Fenian's caves or the longer Oparara track, and definitely walk the Charming Creek either on the way in or out of the area. Make a beach fire. Get clubs at the VisCtr and play golf. Take photos of the Oparara "root beer" river contrasting with the yellow rocks and green ferns. And here's a fun idea…bring something to float on—

Box Canyon Cave ←
Crazy Paving Cave ←

At Oparara Arch

inner tube or raft or something and walk up the Oparara River 3.5 km from the bridge and float back down to the sea. Call it your "root beer float". Study the Topo map and maybe try floating under the arches…a float from one arch to the other...can it be done?? Karamea might have some real adventure up its sleeve—give it a look!

Oparara/ Fenian Track. (I haven't done it, but am excited to do it next time I'm there.) There is now a new-ish track from Moria Gate Arch to the Fenian Track. It's 14km one-way, thus a good day-walk. The trick is that the carparks are 20km apart. If you could park at the Fenian trailhead and then get a shuttle ride up to Oparara, that'd be the best plan. There's no operating shuttle service (yet), due to the paucity of tourists who actually

visit Karamea…but maybe someday. For now, ask at the visitor centre…and maybe you could catch a morning ride up with the Honeycomb Cave guide or simply pay a local for a lift. Near the end of the trek—10km in with 4km to go, you'll cross Fenian Creek and come to the Caves loop. Head 5 more minutes up to the second "Caves" sign, and if you've got a bit of extra energy (and a headlamp) head 6 minutes over to Miner's Cave for a neat look at stalactites galore and a nice showing of glow worms. From there the Fenian track is an easy 4km descent.

Kohaihai Beach/ Heaphy Track. 15km north of Karamea you'll come to the literal "end of the road." The Heaphy Great Walk begins/ends here at the nice beachside free DOC campground. This is the nicest beach area near Karamea. The Kohaihai River forms a huge tannin-stained swimming hole before it charges through a boulder garden to the sea. The beach stretches endlessly south while the Heaphy Track crosses a swingbridge and heads north into the bush. The Heaphy makes an excellent day walk for as far as you feel. There's a mapboard at the campground. The Nikau loop and further to Scott's Beach is a "Great" Heaphy day-walk sampler.

(opah-rarra)

KARAMEA'S CLAIM-TO-FAME SPECTACLES

Walk: easy walks to different sights

- watch YouTube: z0vgj8k1-4g
- bring: flashlights/headlamps for caves and arches

OBSCUR-O-METER

West Coast - NORTH

The Oparara Basin is a pain in the ass to get to, but it has some really cool and unique natural wonders. Near Westport you'll see billboards touting "the largest limestone arches in NZ." Yes, the arches are vast, and the Oparara Arch is so vast that it defies both photography and the title of "arch"—it's SO big that no little promo picture readies you for the WOW! The Moria Gate, while less grandiose, is still no slacker...and a good bit easier to photograph. All the visual splendors of the Oparara Basin are clustered around the one Oparara carpark.

Oparara Arch. The easy 12-minute one-way track to the Oparara Arch follows along the banks of a root-beer stream, with a side path to a small swimming-hole beach. Dare to take a dip in the dark (yet perfectly clean) waters?? Along the way you'll also pass two side streams which will delight photographers with the contrasting green moss/root-beer waterfall combo. The track finally ascends into the MASSIVE archway where the DOC sign tells you "no further." Bring a headlamp so you can see more clearly where you're not supposed to go. Underneath the Oparara Arch is way too cool not to explore, but be sure not to let any boulders fall on your head and kill you. ☺

Inside
Oparara Arch

Small waterfall on Oparara Arch Track

Moria Gate Arch. (Yes, named after LOTR, long before LOTR filmed in NZ!) From the carpark the Moria Gate Arch is 17 minutes along the easy Arch/Tarn 45-minute loop track. **Make sure to bring a headlamp and sandals!** The track, well-graded and easy the entire loop, requires a semi-difficult rock-climbing move to get underneath Moria Arch—you'll need to step down into a rocky pit using a helper-chain, whence you'll emerge under the impressive arch. Super-fun, except if you forget to bring a flashlight and have to try it in the dark. The arch, once you're under-neath, has glow worms underneath and a beach out front—a great place to laze away a bit of afternoon. Aside from the Moria Gate, the rest of the track through the forest is also captivatingly unique, unlike **any other** easily-accessible forest on the South. Giant moss-draped trees preside over an open understory of tree ferns…simply wonderful! From the arch the track continues over the top of the arch then along to a spur out to the Mirror Tarn, then on to the road just a minute up from the carpark.

Box Canyon/ Crazy Paving Stones Caves. These two short caves are 2km up the road from Moria Arch. Both caves share the same entrance track—20 minutes and a headlamp should be sufficient to see them both. Neither will knock your socks off, but both are worth a quick look-see.

Moria Gate Arch

DRIVING: Go 10km north from Karamea towards Kohaihai and turn right at signs for Oparara. Now it's a slow gravel road for 12km to the road-end carparks. There are maps and toilets at the carpark.

West Coast- NORTH

C3 ▶ FENIAN CAVES TRACK

JUNGLE CAVES AND ROOT BEER RIVERS

Walk/Tramp: 4km easy walk one-way w/optional strenuous 1.5km cave-tramping loop

● bring: two headlamps, solid shoes

OBSCURE ▸ POPULAR
OBSCUR-O-METER

Tunnel Cave

The Fenian Track is Karamea's lesser-known alternative to the Oparara Basin. The track is a wide and easy old pack track and it follows the gorgeous root-beer brown Oparara River upstream to access a separate "Caves" loop. The Fenian Track is the end bit of the 14km Oparara Arches/Fenian thru track, so if you wanted you could continue past the caves another 10km to the Oparara arches.

For adventuresome hikers the Fenian Caves are definitely worth a look! The Caves track loops off, then rejoins the main Fenian Track at two signed spots before the Fenian Creek bridge. The loop is a rough and difficult tramping track, best avoided after a heavy rain. The route is marked by DOC arrows but it's still difficult to follow—this is no easy-peasy cave look-see, this is an adventure route!

The Caves loop goes past two caves as well as traversing <u>through</u> "Tunnel Cave" (you cannot complete the caves loop without going thru Tunnel cave, and thus you <u>MUST</u> have headlamps!) Inside each of the

Inside Tunnel Cave

caves there are small running streams....and streams means glow worms. The caves host arrays of stalactites, but don't expect any jaw-drop beauty. Tunnel Cave also sports a large glow worm-lit "picnic room" with a gurgling 3m waterfall which you must climb up to get through and exit the cave. Overall, the glow worms inside Fenian's caves may

76

be the most numerous glow worms in any free public cave on the South Island.

Walk ▶ *(Two lights minimum!)* It's an easy 45 minutes (4km) up the Fenian Track, around Maloney's Bluff, then descending a bit to the first of the two signed "caves" loop entrances. Skip the first junction and head 5 more minutes to the second lower one near the Fenian Creek

Glow worm webs, enlarged (Miner's Cave)

bridge (definitely take a look at this fern-draped, tannin-browned creek). It's best to do the loop clockwise, so you go upstream through Tunnel Cave. Water shoes are NOT necessary—you can get through the caves, other than Cavern Creek, with dry shoes (in fine weather).

Embarking on the marked cave route you'll find Cavern Creek Cave in just 3 minutes—this cave is best to skip since it's slippery and full of sucking knee-deep mud. The marked route bypasses it and goes 20 more minutes of rugged ups 'n' downs to an unmarked short side-cave and then to signed Tunnel Cave. Tunnel Cave is about half-way along the route. Into Tunnel you go, ducking a bit at first before the cave opens up into a large glow

Miner's Cave

worm-festooned waterfall room—a good place to sit in the dark and have a snack! A few minutes past Tunnel Cave is the signed entrance to Miner's Cave. This cave is worth a venture, as it's decorated with a forest of stalactites. You can descend along the cave's stream until the passage squeezes down to a netherworld crawl space—turn back wherever you please. Finally, just a few minutes more and the loop rejoins the main Fenian Track.

Left is back to the carpark, but first it's nice to go (right) down to Fenian Creek, hop down at the bridge, and splash downstream 50m to the midstream boulders where you can rinse the mud off, have a snack, and watch the entire Fenian Creek disappear into a hole!

DRIVING: From Karamea "Market Cross" take the Oparara Rd (not to the beach) 4km to signed Fenian Rd, go right for 1km back past the rock works to the road-end carpark mapboard.

HISTORIC RUINS AND JUNGLY RIVER SCENERY

Walk: easy one-hour (4km) one-way

● watch YouTube: 2-mbbsmuc_q

OBSCUR-O-METER

West Coast - NORTH

Make Time For This Walk!!!!!!!! It's one of the best easy walks on the South Island.

The Charming Creek Walkway is CHARMING^2! This is a walkway through time, through history, through jungle...through beauty. The fairly easy track winds along for about 4km, gaining only 100m the entire way (about 50-60 minutes one-way to Watson's Mill). What you've got here is a track along the long-abandoned Charming Creek railway (which extracted both coal and timber from the surrounding bush.) The walkway follows the actual rails of the railway—you walk between the meter-wide rails the entire walk—as you slowly ascend along the "raging torrent" of the chocolaty-brown Ngakawau River Gorge. This track hosts a bunch of little surprises, as well as a couple of big ones! There's a couple of in-situ relics, a couple of tunnels, a couple of waterfalls, a couple of woo-hoo bridges...and, even a handful of glow worms! All that, and, you'll even read some interesting info panels and learn of the "Exceptionally Busy" Mr. Schadick. For a day-walk a turn-around point at Watson's Mill, just 5 minutes past Mangatini Falls, is a good call.

Historic ore "bins"

Ok, here's a personal appeal from me to everyone reading this book and traveling NZ: Do This Walk! Please. You'll like it. I LOVE it! Make the time, even if you weren't planning to sample Karamea's charms. The 35km drive from Westport is fast and straight, so make the detour. This track, largely ignored by just about everybody, is completely bang-for-the-buck worth it, much more so than some of the over-promoted "highlights" that you'll find farther south on the West Coast. If you like NZ Frenzy by the time you're reading this entry, then just do it for me...I think you'll be glad you did.

Impressive Mangatini Falls

Walk Just follow the rail lines for 4km. No turns or options. Turn back at Watson's Mill (the track continues for many more kms, but not nearly as impressively as the first 4km.

DRIVING: To find the carpark trailhead take SH 67 north from Westport for 35km. At the small township of Ngakawau, turn right at the pub on the south side of the Ngakawau River bridge. Go 500m, crossing the railroad tracks, to the signed carpark.

C5 ▸ MARUIA FALLS VIEW
(mar-ew-ya)

A DRIVE-UP WATERFALL VIEW

Walk: easy 3-minute stroll

● watch YouTube kayak vids: qqyoynkrjpu

OBSCURE   POPULAR

OBSCUR-O-METER

West Coast - NORTH

Maruia Falls is where the wide Maruia River leaps over a 10m escarpment on its mad rush north to join the Buller River. For most folks the falls are just a quick look-see from the fenced viewpoint above the falls. The view there isn't very good though. A much better one is the 3-minute track down to the base of the falls. Maruia Falls change dramatically and quickly depending on the day's rainfall—it's easy for the river to swell more than a meter in just hours...and thus you may see the falls as a raging mist-spewing chocolate-brown torrent, or just a clear gentle-flowing multi-channeled trickle. When the water is low it's fun to hop the viewpoint fence and go down onto the top-o-the-falls rock shelf where the water streams through a spaghetti of channels and fissures. Don't try this at high water, as you'd be surely swept to an untimely (and bad for tourism) death.

High-water Maruia Falls

What's really interesting about Maruia Falls is what the interpretive sign at the falls doesn't tell you, because there isn't one. The neat fact is that Maruia Falls originated due to a catastrophic 1929 earthquake that pummeled the area. A weaker guidebook would simply inform you that the earthquake "caused" the waterfall, leaving you to wonder...how? At first look you may be inclined to wonder if the downstream land dropped away an incredible 10m? But no, a journey into the nearby Murchison Museum's will reveal a file folder filled with newspaper articles detailing that the earthquake caused a massive landslide to the east of the river sending a debris slide into and filling the former river channel, which was roughly underneath the present-day carpark. The earth shook, the land slid, people were crushed…and the river detoured around the landslide pile to establish a new channel through what was a paddock. The museum article details that after one week the new waterfall was about 1m tall, after a few weeks it was 2m, and after a year it was 5m tall. Since about 1947 the falls look as they do now—10m.

Interestingly, the geology article goes on to examine the fact that the existing waterfall existed prior to earthquake-caused re-birth! Evidence indicates that an Ice-Age debris-flow covered up a pre-historic Maruia Falls, re-routing the river channel…and this pre-historic waterfall only re-asserted itself after the 1929 landslide dammed-up the then-channel, letting the river rediscover its former waterfall! Whew, how did Tourism NZ pass up this opportunity to tout "a world-famous earthquake re-engineered Jurassic waterfall"???? Hopefully DOC will come to its senses and have Christchurch writer/satirist Joe Bennett pen a fun info plaque ode to this peculiar not-quite-yet Tourist Attraction.

Exploring low-water Falls

DRIVING: The signed Maruia Falls carpark is on SH 65, 11km south of the SH 6 junction west of Murchison, or 60km north of Springs Junction.

WESTPORT'S SCENIC MUST-SEE

Walk: rugged, rock-hopping 1.0 km one-way

• bring: tide chart, water sandals, swim/
  birthday suit

OBSCUR-O-METER

West Coast - NORTH

WALKWAY TO GIBSONS BEACH

CAUTION REQUIRED ON STEEP TRACK

ACCESS HAS BEEN KINDLY
PROVIDED BY HOLCIM
Holcim

The Cape Foulwind lighthouse may be the least appealing lighthouse in New Zealand. Pass the smokestacks, dodge the massive cement-loading trucks on their way to/from the lighthouse's neighbor quarry...and you're there—just a 500m walk to see the not-too-engaging sight. You can walk the bluff-top track from lighthouse to the seal colony—it's about 3km one-way, but not too exciting. Ignoring that option, maybe drive south to see the seal colony at Tauranga Bay. Ugh. You'll only get a distant view of some seals from too-crowded small view platforms... probably the least interesting seal colony on the island. As much as I like seal pups, I cannot deal with a crowded platform with snap-happy tourists jostling for a crappy telephoto of a lazing seal. The only reason tourists flock to this site is because it is the first one many have seen if they've come south via the ferry. Save your time and pixels for elsewhere.

Cape Foulwind
Lighthouse/carpark

Surprise!   Low-tide access

So, all's foul at Foulwind right...sounds like I dislike the place and maybe you should skip it and hurry south to the pancakes or north to Abel Tasman? Nope. If you happen (or plan) on a low tide at the Cape Foulwind lighthouse's carpark, you may be fortunate enough to stumble onto the sign announcing the HOLCIM-courtesy track down to Gibsons Beach. Look south and you may be intrigued by all the odd-looking rocks, tidal shelves, and distant mud-stone cliffs. If you're so lucky (or well-planned) to take a walk down to the beach...hey whoa, a waterfall....then, whoa, some weird rocks looking like sea-rounded bould-ers nestled like eggs in a carton against the ribbed mudstone layers. Then there's more.

Beach Archway

Here's what to do...wear a swimsuit and sandals, and walk 10 minutes. Whoa, two archway tunnels lead thigh-deep through the headland, onto, whoa, a secret beach. Keep heading and rock-hop over to the next hidden sandy cove. WHOA, even better!! Hope you brought your birthday suit! I love waterfall showers spitting off seaside cliffs.....do you??

This 1.0km slice of low-tide is a total unexpected adventure. Since I've now told you about it a little, I may have spoiled some surprise, but I think you'll still LOVE it! **LOW-TIDE only.** Get it? There's nothing to see and nowhere to go mid-tide or higher. Expect no footprints but your own...because the beaten tourist track leads over to the lighthouse, then to the seals. This li'l hidden nugget coast is for the other folks, folks like you, folks venturing off the Tourism path.

If you enjoyed Wharariki (A1), then you'll like Gibsons. If you like Gibsons, you'll LOVE the North Island's Tongaporutu (cover photo of NZ Frenzy North).

Walk ▶ Down road, over rocks, past waterfall, over tidal shelves, thru arch, across beach, get wet! Repeat in reverse. Make sure to inspect the grey mudstone cliff wall for prolific fossils on the way back.

Fossil rocks

DRIVING: Head 15 km towards Cape Foulwind from Westport. The Gibsons signed track is just before the main carpark.

STALACTITE—FILLED HISTORIC CAVE TUNNEL

Tramp: moderate 60 minute (3.5km) one-way to cave

● bring: 2 lights/headlamps, watershoes for river crossings

OBSCUR-O-METER

A one-hour tramping track heads upstream paralleling the Fox River to access the historic Fox River Cave. The track requires fording the ankle-to-thigh deep Fox River (depending on rainfall) twice. Solid water shoes are the best bet for both the track and the puddle-prone cave.

The cave has been a tourist draw since 1906, as you'll read on info panel mounted at the cave mouth. Nowadays the cave is well worth a look…, but only if you really like caves. If you're not too interested in the underground world, then skip this track and head for the more scenic Pororari River Canyon (C10).

For cave lovers, the Fox River Cave stands proud. It's well decorated and by NZ public-cave standards and it hasn't been defaced or defiled much—no walls full of writings nor rows of chopped-off stalactites. The 200m cave tunnel features plenty of delicacy, especially the groves of soda straws with some two feet long! This cave is a bit unique in that it wasn't pillaged of its delicate wonders by NZ pioneers, but rather "saved" as a tourist attraction said to rival Waitomo "back in the day". In reality it doesn't rival Waitomo in the least, but it's still worth the jungly tramp to go see it.

Two river crossings enroute to cave

Inside "decorated" cave

Tramp ▶ From the seaside carpark at the Fox River mouth it's about 35 minutes until the first river ford, and then the second crossing is just minutes later. At the signed junction for the Inland Pack Track, go left and the cave is about another 18 minutes up steep slippery rocks to the impressive cave mouth.

DRIVING: The signed carpark on SH 6 is on the north side of the Fox River bridge, 12km north of the Punakaiki blowholes or 19km south of Charleston.

West Coast - NORTH

UNBELIEVABLE NATURAL SPECTACLE!!

Walk: short, easy viewpoint loop walk

- watch Meet the Locals: "Pancake Rocks"
- watch YouTube: Litf9hdwj34

OBSCUR-O-METER

West Coast - NORTH

The famed "Pancake rocks" are a Westland experience not to be missed!! Regrettably, hordes of travelers "miss" them every day. If you

aren't out at Dolomite Point—the Blowholes—at or near HIGH TIDE, then you've missed the whole point of visiting. At low/mid tide the rocks are a bunch of layered limestone only worthy of a 5-second photo-op. At HIGH TIDE though—watch out, as Punakaiki comes alive like a rumbling monster!

When the seas are running big, as you near the viewpoints on the short paved pathway, you'll begin to feel the ground shake and the deep bass tones of underground cavern exploding with wave surge. Punakaiki has a tremendous "feel"...so much more than all photos can show! The sea whooshes as it surges into the corrugated limestone slots, hisses as it begins to blow, then BOOMS an eruption of cascading seawater! Seconds later a mist of salty spray will tickle everyone on the view platform with its briny kiss. Completely Fabulous...if you're there at **HIGH TIDE!!!** Patience is a must at the blowholes since the waves come in sets—give yourself a minimum of 45 minutes out at the various viewpoints. The waves come in sets, and if you leave one view for another before the first one puts on its BIG BOOM, then all you'll hear is the crowd behind you gasping in applause.

Photographers should definitely bring some sort of lens cloth and maybe a small towel to quickly cover your camera when the blowhole really blows. While you cover your lens from the hard-to-clean-off salt spray... open your mouth and let your tongue taste Punakaiki's salty mists. Yum.

Carpark Visitor Center signage

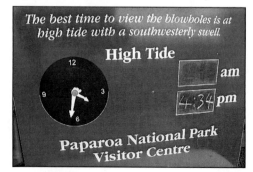

The best time to view the blowholes is at high tide with a southwesterly swell.

High Tide

12

9   3

6

am

4:34 pm

Paparoa National Park Visitor Centre

Blowhole tourists

PLAN YOUR TRIP AROUND HIGH TIDE! Wherever you're coming from, check the news-paper for the high tide time at either Westport or Greymouth. There's plenty to do nearby to Punakaiki at low tide—that's when the beaches are good…and at mid tide it's time to explore a river or cave. Don't come all the way to Punakaiki and miss out on high tide. Plan ahead or all you'll experience is a dull look at striated rock instead of an explosive spectacle of Neptune's fury!

WOW!

DRIVING: The Paparoa/Punakaiki DOC VisCtr is located on SH 6 about 45km north of Greymouth or 60 km south of Westport. The VisCtr will have high tides times posted at the front door if you haven't planned ahead much.

A SCULPTED PUNAKAIKI BEACH COVE

Walk: easy 10-minute (1.0 km) to cove

- watch YouTube: mqwairszqgk
- bring: a swimsuit and camera, tide chart

OBSCURE POPULAR
OBSCUR-0-METER

West Coast - NORTH

The Truman track is a short track to a small low-tide-only beach that's overlooked by most visitors to Paparoa in their haste to see the blowholes and then hurry on. Don't miss the Truman track. Though it's short, it packs a scenic punch larger than its length. First, the track itself is an

Waterfall

Truman Cove (low-tide)

easy and delightful 10 minutes through very jungly Westland rainforest. Ferns and palms and moss and scraggly trees form a rainforest tunnel down to the beach, all highlighted by a bunch of good interpretive signs. The track ends on a rock shelf overlooking the Truman cove where at higher tides the wave bash and splash and blow a bit. The better time to visit is at half-tide or lower when you can take the steps down to the cove onto the sand to explore (you should be at the Pancake Rocks at high tide.) What you'll find in Truman's

Truman Beach Waterfall

cove is a small waterfall pouring off a wave-eroded limestone overhang directly onto the beach! It's fairly unique for a waterfall to actually pour off a cliff onto the sand, and you won't find many like it anywhere in New Zealand. On the North Island there are many waterfalls that sort of dribble and bounce down sheer cliffs onto the sand, but never one like Truman's that takes a big leap. Bring a bathing suit, because if your boyfriend is decent with a camera, you can get a great photo-memory of taking a beach shower under a sculpted Punakaiki cliff!!

DRIVING: The Truman Track has a signed carpark on SH 6, 2.5km north of the blowholes.

(porro-rarry)

A SCENIC LIMESTONE RIVER CANYON WALK

Walk: easy 45-minute (3.5 km) one-way to Pack track jct.

• bring: swimsuit

OBSCUR-O-METER

Pororari River

West Coast- NORTH

This Pororari River track is a mostly-easy 45-minutes one-way walk through a wonderful limestone river canyon festooned with jungly sub-tropical rainforest on downstream end and temperate Beech forest on the upstream reaches—a neat transition. The obvious highlight of the track is the river itself. The Pororari, depending on rain, can either be a clear languidly-flowing invitation to walkers to leap into any of its many boulder-framed emerald pools...or, during rain, it can be a frothing muddy beast on a barely-controlled hurtle through the jungle. Either mood the Pororari is in is sure to please—give it a look!

The track contours the river bank, generally a few meters above the river. There are a couple sets of steps over/under some boulders, but otherwise it's easy-walking for the entire family. The day-walk ends at the Inland Pack Track junction, where the Pack Track descends to a small beach on the Pororari (the Pack Track continues either north or south into the adjacent river canyons if you wanted a much longer loop route to try—get info at the i-Site if so.)

So, for the shorter day-walk, turn back where the Pack Track descends left to the river just a few hundred meters from the junction sign. On the way back along the Pororari Track take time to leave the track and scamper down to the riverside rock gardens because the magnificent canyon walls are better viewed from the river than the track.

Jungly walking track

DRIVING: The signed Pororari carpark is 1km north of the blowholes.

THE SOUTH'S MOST SCENIC BEACH WALK

Walk: 3km one-way

- bring: tide chart, water sandals
- watch YouTube: bfsmifz0vva

OBSCURE   POPULAR

OBSCUR-O-METER

West Coast - NORTH

Plan Ahead!! Low-Tide <u>ONLY</u>! Most every tourist on the South island has passed this short stretch of coast, but few stop, as few know about this coastline wonder-walk. The Motukiekie Coast, short as it is, may be the South Island's MOST DRAMATIC bit of walkable coast!!!!!* Motukiekie is oft-featured on panoramic postcards, but the photographers don't tell you where this dramatic slice of scenery is located. I will.

Lemme try again in case I wasn't clear. NOWHERE on this South Island will you find a more interesting, photogenic, and WOW section of beach that you can actually walk. The reason you've never heard of it on any of those brochure maps or i-Site rubbish is that it's free, hard to access, needs planning…and nobody has commercialized it!

Even more so than Punakaiki, where knowing when high tide happens is helpful, knowing low-tide at Motukiekie is **imperative**—no low-tide, no beach walk. If it ain't low, you can't go!!

What Motukiekie's got here, decorating this little-visited stretch of coast 20km north of Greymouth, is an offshore sea-stack cornucopia, high cliffs and arches and caves and waterfalls and corrugated tidal shelving. Motukiekie at low tide is fricking amazing!! Every month is different at Motukiekie, every day is different!! Each week the tides and Westland storms bring and/or remove heaps of sand and pebbles from Motukiekie, either hiding or revealing the fascinatingly brain-like tidal shelf…and, given

Motu = island
kiekie = shrub

Motukiekie Point Archway

Westland's weather, the rain is probably either pouring or drizzling, thus yielding waterfalls gushing off cliffs and rushing across beach, or mere trickles festooning the fern-draped heights. Another bit of interest on this beach is the rusting collection of cars that have plunged to their deaths from the highway above—yikes.

Here's why Motukiekie sees few foreign visitors. Most folks are tourists —they bumble around NZ hoping to "see the sights" without expending much effort to find the truly unique uncommercialized spots. Travelers, on the other hand, are fewer. Travelers attempt to find good info about wonderful spots and experiences. Motukiekie is one of those spots. You gotta know where, you gotta know when…and you gotta PLAN AHEAD. Hope to see ya there!!

Hike ► From the roadside car parking, the walk is simple—find a gully down onto the beach then head south towards the sea stacks. But, here's the rub—the sea blocks the way as it bashes the cliffs, <u>except within 1.5 hours of low-tide.</u> So first, figure out when Greymouth's low-tide is from any newspaper's tide charts. Next, plan to begin the walk south on a falling tide only, about 1.5-2 hours before low-tide. The best walk takes about an hour to get to the other side of the seastack point for a look from the other direction (and to see all the caves, arches, waterfalls, etc). At mid-tide you could walk for about 20 minutes and maybe make it to the double arch point, but that'd be just an awful tease. Make a good plan…you'll have the beach to yourself as the tourists just don't know, and they won't be told.

Rusting cliffside car wrecks

*Abel Tasman may argue, as may Curio Bay (F6), Whariki Beach (A1), and Kaikoura (A15) but those places are in Lonely Planet and mobbed…come see Motukiekie, just you and your camera!

DRIVING: From Greymouth head north on SH 6 for 20km, and 3.7km north of the "Twelve-Mile" hairpin bridge, slow as you descend the hill and pull off left at the first left-side pulloff past the cottages.

From Punakaiki go south on SH 6 for 24km and as you drive along the dramatic coast, pass 13-Mile Creek and in 500m pull off right before Kararoa Creek bridge. If you get to some cottages, you've gone a little too far.

C12 COAL CREEK FALLS

A PHOTOGRAPHER'S OFF-THE-BEATEN-TRACK WALERFALL

Walk: easy/mod 20-minute one-way (2 km)

• bring: water sandals, swimsuit, tripod

OBSCUR-0-METER

West Coast - NORTH

Coal Creek Falls Walk
1 hour return

Coal Creek Falls is a small waterfall at the end of a mile-long bush track. This isn't a waterfall that'll make anyone's NZ top-ten list, yet, for some, it may warrant a stop. If you're traveling and maybe a bit tired of the tourist-a-go-go from either the Fox/Franz/Hokitika hustle or the Pancakie tourist posse, then detour off the Westland highway and go for a nice deep-forest walk to a out-of-the-way spot where there are NO tourists.

Low-water day

Coal Creek Falls itself is about 7m high and 20m wide, and the look of the falls varies widely depending on the week's rain (my pix are low-water from a no-rain week.) There's a dark pool of tannin-stained water below the falls which local kids love on hot summer days.

Photographers will like this waterfall. There are a bunch of angles to play with, foreground rock combinations, macro close-up potentials, and even the chance to capture the waterfall's reflection if the pool is still. Bring a tripod that you can set up in a bit of shallow water, and also bring water-sandals so you can rock-hop to some different spots. The rock that Coal Creek Falls spill over has a reddish tinge that nicely contrasts the green algae/moss.

When it's grey in Greymouth, Coal Creek Falls makes a good walk. It's 20-minutes on a fairly easy track through forest and bush...lots of cicadas, few people. If you're waiting for a low-tide at Motukiekie, this is a good way to spend the time.

DRIVING: 7km north of Greymouth's river bridge is Runanga town. In the middle of town turn east (right) at the Coal Creek Falls sign onto Seddon St and follow it 1km (with one right turn) to the signed road-end carpark.

MINING RUINS, RELICS, AND TUNNELS

Walk: various easy explorations

● Google: "DOC Brunner Mine"

OBSCUR-O-METER

West Coast - NORTH

Brunner Industrial Site. The Brunner mining site is super easy and fast to visit. You'll see massive 1800s coal mine workings, ruins and relics. Interestingly, the extensive ruins here are "restored ruins," meaning that they were unearthed from the encroaching kiwi bush just 30 years ago. The site features a one-hour self-guided walk touring a chimney, mineshafts, oven works…and a scenic bridge across the Grey River. Interpretive signs and a paper pamphlet enliven the history—learn about the god-awful living conditions and the hellish "Barber", as well as tragic 1896 explosion that killed everyone underground. (Under the bridge is a swimming-hole picnic spot.)

Brunner

Drive: The Brunner site is signed 11km from Greymouth on SH 7.

Brunner Bridge

Nelson Creek. Nelson Creek is an old gold-mining boom town, now a camping and recreation site. Nelson Creek has a riverside free (donation) camping ground, a swimming hole, and a few short, interesting loop tracks. The swimming hole in the tannin-stained creek has a popular jumping rock for local kids—up the rope you go for a splash-down! A mapboard at the campground details the walking tracks as well as summarizing the interesting gold-mining history of the area. The tracks begin with a fun zigzag through a tunnel and then across a looooong swingbridge. The Tailrace loop features an interesting optional tunnel exploration (bring a torch), while the Colls Dam loop has a heap of bridges, each bridge spanning some peculiarly impressive man-made mining tailrace slot canyons—very weird!

Drive: Nelson Creek Rd is 25km NE from Greymouth on SH 7, just past Ngahere. Turn right for 6.5km then turn left into the park adjacent to the pub.

Nelson Tunnel

Goldsborough DOC campground. 25km south of Greymouth (10km south of Kumara Junction), turn at signs and go 8km to site. Goldsborough is a basic $6 DOC camp with flush toilets and walking tracks. A mapboard details the routes. The Tunnel Terrace walk, signed 2km before the campground, is short and brilliant. Tunnels both begin and end this interesting loop…and bring a torch to explore the mystery tunnel in the middle.

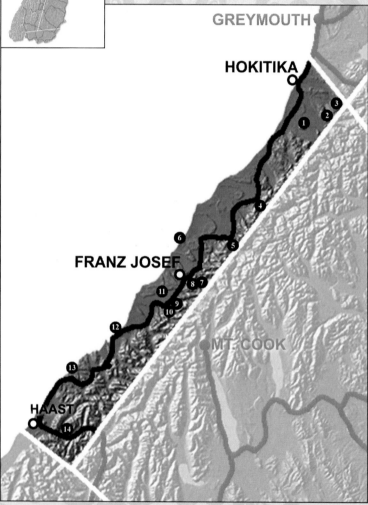

D1 Hokitika Gorge
D2 Lake Kaniere/Dorothy Falls
D3 Cesspool of Arahura River
D4 Amethyst Hot Springs
D5 Whataroa River
D6 Okarito Beach Track
D7 Franz Josef Glacier

D8 Robert's Point Track
D9 Fox Glacier Valley
D10 Fox's Chalet Track
D11 Fox's Lake Matheson
D12 Bruce Bay/Maori Beach
D13 Monro Beach Track
D14 Haast Pass

WEST COAST - SOUTH

The southern half of Westland is where the grandeur of the Southern Alps impressively towers over the West Coast rainforest jungle. **Very Impressive!** Sadly, it rains in buckets in these parts and most travelers on hurried South Island itineraries speed through the area, rarely hanging around long enough to give the clouds a chance to part in order to reveal the majestic snow-capped peaks rising above the iconic glaciers. These two glaciers, Franz Josef and Fox, are undoubtedly the scenic highlight of the entire West Coast. Both these glacier-named towns are deservedly popular, so expect full carparks, plenty of tour buses, and nearly 100% tourism-orientation. Regardless of the Heli-tour hoopla, these glaciers are unique in the world and easily accessible whether you're a keen tramper or drive-by sight-seer.

The main town of interest in this area of the coast is Hokitika. Hokitika is still a small Kiwi town that does a good job of attracting travelers without selling-out its small-town soul. Hokitika has fashioned itself as the Greenstone/Jade capitol of NZ, as well as the artsy beach driftwood capitol.

Of special note is the tiny village of Okarito. Aside from its wonderful Southern Alps skyline panorama, it may be the only chance most South Island travelers have at spotting an actual Kiwi bird on the local Ranger-lead night-time walks. If you're keen on Kiwis and not bound for Stewart Island, then Okarito is your best bet to see an oh-so-rare Kiwi.

Haast Pass is the island's "waterfall pass" leaving the wet coast for the much drier and sunnier (and sandfly-free) Wanaka/Queenstown areas. The SH 6 road is curvy and slow-going, but gorgeous the entire way, especially after heavy rain. If you're sick and tired of Westland's sandflies, welcome relief awaits at Lake Wanaka on the far side of the pass. On the other hand, if you're heading west from Wanaka, you better be armed with DEET (see Appendix 1).

D

Don't miss:
    Glaciers (7-11)
    Hokitika Gorge (1)

D1 ▶ HOKITIKA GORGE
(Hoe-ka-tick-a)

SURREAL BLUE WATER

Walk: short, easy 7-minute stroll

● watch YouTube: wnzctLmL6ha

OBSCUR-O-METER

Visitors to Hokitika often combine a visit to Hokitika Gorge and Lake Kaniere into a long 80km-driving outing. It's probably best to see the Gorge first, and then plan to spend more time around the lake relaxing if the weather's fine.

The Hokitika Gorge is a long drive—33km—from Hokitika, so the question is, "is the photo-op worth it?" Yes is the easy answer, especially if you are coming from the north. Even on a grey drizzly day the Gorge's colors are impressive. There are many powder-blue rivers in the south of the South Island, but none more easily photographed than Hokitika's Gorge. The water is an otherworldly milky opaque blue due to suspended glacier-ground "rock flour". It's the same eerie blue as Lakes Pukaki/Tekapo and rivers just to the south like Whataroa/Haast. What makes Hokitika Gorge so special is that the water pools up and is penned-in by grey rocks for a 300m stretch, all surrounded by verdant green bush and spanned by a scenic swingbridge. This makes the scene super-easy to photograph and appreciate. It's almost impossible to take a bad photo of Hokitika Gorge, and when you get home, it'll be the kind of photo that you'll show others to make them salivate over your NZ trip.

There's not much to do at the Gorge than just look. From the carpark an easy track heads 7 minutes over to the swingbridge, and from there

you can scramble down to the rocks and water for a quick icy splash. There are no other walks or anything else to explore nearby.

DRIVING: A local map from the i-Site is a big help. In Hokitika on SH 6 turn at the signs for Kaniere Lake and Hokitika Gorge. In about 5km you'll turn right to go to the Gorge, then follow signs zig-zagging through the farm lands.

D2 ▸ LAKE KANIERE/DOROTHY FALLS

(kaan-ee-err)

SWIMMING/BOATING LAKE WITH A WATERFALL

Walk: short walks

• various drive-up access points

OBSCUR-O-METER

Lake Kaniere

Lake Kaniere is a natural lake set amidst bush-clad hills with some distant views of snow-capped peaks. There are a number of lake-access points around the lake and a DOC campground at the NE end (Hans Bay–$6pp). The 2WD gravel road around the east side of the lake is kept in good condition. The north end of the lake is more popular with water-skiers and such, while the south end near Dorothy Falls is more quiet and mellow.

Dorothy Falls are signed along the east-side road and for most people the 30m falls make for a quick photo-stop. Scrambling adventurers may see that there's an upper portion to the falls just barely visible from the bottom. Dorothy's drop is listed at 64m…and that's a lot more than you see at the bottom, so…hmmm, maybe there's a lot more falls hidden above. Go see…a rough path investigates the tops.

The lake access path at Dorothy Falls provides some of the nicest swimming on the lake. Surprisingly, this lake warms up during a rare spell of hot west coast weather. The brown waters of Kaniere are a tannin-stained (from the ferns), but the water is clean.

Upper Dorothy Falls

FYI ▸ For a unique trip through the Hokitika area you can see 3 oddly different types of water in a day—Hokitika Gorge's milky blue, Kaniere's tannin browned, and then Cesspool's crystal-clear aquamarine. Ya won't find that combo many places on Earth!

DRIVING: It's best to check a local map from the i-Site. From Hokitika the lake is 18km. Just north of town turn east on the signed road and follow it to the lake.

If you are coming from Hokitika Gorge, turn in Kokatahi at signs for the lake to get to the south end of shoreline road.

REMOTE RIVER SWIMMING HOLE

Walk: easy/mod 25-minute one-way (2 km)

● bring: swimsuit, picnic, bug spray

OBSCURE   POPULAR

OBSCUR-O-METER

West Coast · SOUTH

By definition a cesspool is "a sewage pit or morally disgusting place". The Cesspool Gorge on the upper Arahura River in no way resembles that definition. Maybe, in some long-ago NZ time, this river gorge was trashed by mining and such...but nowadays the river runs pure, though stuck with the uninviting name. The Cesspool Gorge, reached via a long drive from Hokitika and then a short walk, is a fabulous swimming hole on the crystal-blue Arahura. Making the scene even more interesting is an old-timey swingbridge spanning the gorge—one of the older ones without wood planking, just wiring...making for a real swinger! The pool is rimmed with boulders to sun on/leap from and there are also sandy and grassy areas beside the river to picnic/sun/hang out. Of course, a sunny day sure helps to enjoy a swimming hole in Westland—if it's grey out the Cesspool won't be too scenic or inviting.

The Cesspool swingbridge is just the beginning of the multi-day Arahura/ Styx Rivers tramp, so feel free to continue the track upriver for however long you'd like before turning back, (or 4-5 days if you feel so inclined). Formerly the Cesspool area was the carpark for the multi-day tramp, but most of the final 2km of the road has washed out and become a walking track. Thus, the Cesspool is nowadays even more private because you have to walk a bit on the old road to get to it instead of driving directly to it.

Cesspool Swing Bridge
1 Person Maximum Load

Arahura Cesspool

FYI ▶ For a quick 'n' easy overnight backpack outing, the Cesspool makes a good destination—plenty of grassy areas for tents and morning sun to chase away the sandflies.

Walk ▶ Walk up and down the eroded road bed until it deposits you at the riverside swimming hole and swingbridge area. The track up to the bridge starts at a DOC arrow just back up the road a few meters from the riverside area.

If you see some locals poking around (fossicking) in the riverbed, they're most likely looking for Pounamu (Greenstone), which the river is justifiably famous for. Keep your eyes peeled and you find your own hunk of rare Greenstone treasure.

DRIVING: From Hokitika drive 18km to Lake Kaniere. Just past the Canoe Creek area near the northern lakeshore, turn left onto gravel Milltown Rd. Follow this 10km through the scenic Arahura Valley until you cross the Arahura River bridge. Just after the bridge you'll see a heavy-duty iron gate on the right which you need to open and go through. The gate is heavy and difficult to get open, but it does function—pull the big "pin" to start. Once through bump-bump along the road 2km to the grassy riverside area just before the road wash-out (if you can't get the gate open you'll have to walk the extra 2km.)

A SMALL SANDY HOT NATURAL POOL

Walk: easy 12-minute one-way (1.0 km)

• bring: bug spray for sandflies, digging shovel

OBSCURE — POPULAR
OBSCUR-O-METER

Amethyst Stream mouth

Hot Pool

West Coast · SOUTH

Wanganui River carpark view

Amethyst Hot Springs, along with Sylvia Flats, are the only easy-to-reach natural hot springs on the South Island. Also like Sylvia Flats (B5) these springs are along a flood-prone river bank and the quality of the pools depends on the enthusiasm of the digger-outers. Unlike Sylvia Flats though, very few mainstream guidebook authors, and thus few travelers, know of the existence of the Amethyst hot pools. Every winter the Wanganui River floods and re-engineers its channel, recently washing away the road where you now park. By the time you're reading this the river and the path may have changed again and the pools may have been swamped under a new load of sand. Whether the Amethyst hot pools are "good" is anyone's guess, but at least it doesn't take a long detour to investigate. Hope these pix can direct you fairly well to find the hot pool, and at least the entire adventure is only minutes off the main Westland SH 6 travel route…Go See!

What you get, at least as of Feb 2010, is a sandy two-person shoveled-out hot pool—too hot for a sunny day, but perfect in typical Westland grey. It's best to bring some sort of digging implement with you, even if it's just a traveler's cooking pan. At dusk and dawn sandflies WILL definitely swarm, as well as on grey days. You Are Warned! Just like at Sylvia Flats though, the sandflies go to bed at dark leaving just you, your mermaid, a box of wine, and the Southern Cross rising over the mountains. If you visit by day, even if the springs are too hot, the huge sandy riverbed "beach" surrounding the pools makes a great place to play Frisbee, skip stones, and lessen your tan lines.

The Amethyst hot pool area is also perfect short overnight tent outing— just set up camp on the huge sandbar (of course, not when rain pours and flood threatens). There's heaps of available driftwood for a nice night of hot-pool 'n' bonfire riversong serenity.

Pssst, nobody tell Lonely Planet about this spot!

Walk ▶ From the road-end "Wanganui Valley" sign head straight for the river then follow the user-path along the top of the bluff where the road was washed away. The springs are just 1km ahead along the sandy left bank of the river. Go through some bush and then onto the "closed" road for a few hundred meters to the Amethyst Stream bridge. Cross the bridge and go <u>exactly 200m</u> and look for the path on the right leading quickly down to the Wanganui Riverbed. At the riverbed the springs are to the right (downstream), halfway to mouth of the Amethyst Stream, tucked next to the bush line. (As you emerge from the path to the riverbed, make sure to take a look back so you can find the path on the way out—it's easy to misplace.)

Author at work

West Coast- SOUTH

DRIVING: On SH 6, 5km north of Harihari, on the north side of the Wanganui River bridge, turn upstream on the unsigned road and go just 1km until the road ends at the wash out (with the private gate on the left.)

Coming from the north the Wanganui Bridge is about 11km south of Lake Ianthe.

D5 ▶ WHATAROA RIVER
(faata-row-a)

A RIVER OF CAR–STOPPING BLUE

Walk: easy, short sightseeing walk

- discount glacier flights
- watch YouTube: qbb5q9b2kLa

OBSCUR-O-METER

The Whataroa River often runs remarkably blue. BLUE to make you slow the car while crossing the bridge, BLUE to make you park and gawk! Not just BLUE though, there's also a backdrop of jagged grey snow-capped peaks and a helicopter waiting to whisk you up and around the heights. If you're coming from the North, this BLUE is like that of the Hokitika Gorge…simply eye-boggling! If you've yet to witness Lake Tekapo, Lake Pukaki or any of the famed Southland glacial rivers, then the Whataroa River is a glimpse of the eye candy that awaits as you tour southwards.

The BLUE may stop you, but make sure to turn up the short road on the south side of the bridge. Have a splash in the BLUE there at the carpark, but also check-out this helicopter's rates for a glacier flight. All I can say is that it's a way cheaper flight than you'll find in the upcoming glacier tourist-a-ramas, and you get a fly-over this amazing BLUE river to boot. This is probably the most old-school, non-touristy-feeling glacier flight operation in the glacier area (Glacier Country Scenic Flights).

OK, enough commercialized promotion, (I've received nothing for this, nor have I actually taken the flight…but the travelers I met loved their flights). For an even better photo of the Whataroa River and the mountain backdrop than the one you've undoubtedly already taken from the carpark, ask the Heli-man for permission to walk up the signed farm track. Just 5 minutes up the track the photo-op becomes smashingly better, and you may spy an elusive Okarito white heron on the way.

Southern Alps over the Whataroa River

Upriver White Heron

DRIVING: The Whataroa Bridge is 36km north of Franz Josef... also a few km north of Whataroa town, or 26km south of Harihari.

D6 ▶ OKARITO BEACH LOOP ROUTE
(oka-reeto)

VIEW—PACKED BEACH/BLUFFS LOOP WALK

Walk: moderate 2-hour beach and bluffs loop walk (7km round-trip)

- watch Meet the Locals: "Rarest Kiwi"
- bring: tide chart, Kiwi bird curiosity

OBSCUR-O-METER

Okarito often gets tourism publicity for its commercial Okarito Lagoon tours and kayak rentals as well as the night-time Kiwi bird tours where you can actually **see a live Kiwi bird in the wild!** These one-of-a-kind night-time tours, led by a dedicated local Kiwi-conservationist, cost about $60pp, which is way cheaper than a trip to Stewart Island. (The North Island has two such opportunities to see a Kiwi in the wild…at Trounson Park and Aroha Island, both in my North guidebook.)

Much lesser-known about Okarito is its excellent beach 'n' bluffs loop track. The track heads south from the road-end Okarito beach carpark. **The beach portion of the loop is only accessible half-tide or lower.** Thankfully, DOC posts a low-tide time chart on their sign at the beach carpark. The beach walk is under the bluffs for about 45 minutes (3km) to Three-Mile Lagoon, and then the forested bluff walk is a more strenuous 50 minutes (3.5km) back to the carpark with plenty of ups and downs along the age-old miner's pack track.

What Tourism Okarito fails to tells the world, because possibly few people ever get to see it (given that it rains here 110% of the time)…is that on a clear day the 180° panoramic view looking south over the 3-Mile Lagoon bridge is the finest on the West Coast! Whoa, substantial claim, but here's the details; first, the foreground is a scenic bridge crossing the

West Coast· SOUTH

Under-the-bluff beach

dark waters of jungle-clad 3-Mile Lagoon. Above the lagoon to the east an array of snow-capped Alps dazzle, showing the top snowfields of the Franz Josef Glacier and the peaks of Mt Tasman and Mt Cook. To complete the scene, looking SW, a driftwood-strewn beach and turquoise sea stretch endlessly south to Gillespies Point. Yup, Mtn tops to deep sea, glacier to lagoon—pray for a clear day,

cuz this is the best viewpoint the West Coast offers...and one few people or other guidebooks seem to know about!!

Walk ► You gotta time the tide. If you're within 2 hours of low-tide, then hurry along the beach rout—the "pinch point" is half way. If the tide is high, take the high route and maybe check-in on the Trig en route. You could do the bluffs route as an out/back if the tide is high...or, when you get to 3-Mile Lagoon bridge, you could spend some time walking south on the long beach over there until the tide ebbs enough to allow you back along the beach under the bluffs.

FYI ► Camping. Okarito has a little-publicized but nice community campground near the driftwood-strewn beach, about $10pp with hot showers for a dollar. This camp is popular with some of the "off-the-beaten-path" adventure tour bus groups who try to avoid the Franz/Fox mob scene.

FJ Glacier   Mt. Tasman   Mt. Cook

DRIVING: Okarito is signed from SH 6 between Whataroa and Franz Josef, then 10km down the paved road.

THE BETTER GLACIER VALLEY WALK

Walk: easy 30 minute (2.5 km) one-way

- watch YouTube: 06y7h8qdyyu & h9xqLqL1yfu
- bring: swimsuit, sandals

OBSCURE   POPULAR

OBSCUR-O-METER

Roberts Pt (D8)

Waterfall Shower

Franz Josef Glacier Valley

West Coast - SOUTH

The Franz Josef Glacier Valley walk is the more interesting of the two glacier valley walks, and it seems less crowded since tourists are spread out over a longer distance than at Fox Glacier. It takes an easy 30 minutes from the carpark to reach the roped-off end of the track some 200m before the glacier's snout. Along the way there are a bunch of waterfalls in side canyons and a very photogenic triple falls directly on the track. Red-blossomed Southern Rata trees adorn the towering canyon walls in the summertime. Sheer jagged walls tower overhead and you get a good look up the face of FJ's canyon-filling ice field as you walk towards it. At the track's end near the crumbling nose of the glacier you'll get a good look at the cave from whence pours the icy Waiho River. Ropes and signs prevent people from attempting to get closer to the wall of ice (people have died getting too close and having ice chunks "knock 'em cold"). Often you'll also see parties of guided glacier-walkers making their way down the hyper-steep front face of the gravel-covered portion of the snout.

If you're the type for wacky off-the-beaten-path ideas, then wear a bathing suit under your regular clothes for this track. The scenic triple waterfall that tumbles down the canyon wall about half-way to the glacier, surprisingly, isn't ice cold—it's the "temperate" part of this wondrously unique glacier/rainforest combo that makes this area so special in the world (it's a

FJ's Waiho River

rain-fed waterfall rather than an ice-melt flow). So, what better way to celebrate NZ's unique marvels than to strip down to your swimsuit and then have a bit of a waterfall shower—in sight of the frozen wall of ice! Where else in the world can you do this and not be freezing cold?? The left-most of the three waterfalls even has a dry photo spot where your friends can take some memorable pix. Woo-hooo, Fun at the Franz!

Glacier

Waterfall shower!

DRIVING: Franz's glacier access is signed at the south end of the river bridge, just south of Franz Josef town.

D8 **ROBERT'S POINT, FRANZ JOSEF GLACIER**
GLACIERLAND'S BEST DAY-WALK TRACK

Tramp: strenuous 2 hours (5-6 km) one-way
- watch YouTube: p6bfuyirvLe
- elevation Waiho River: 200m
- elevation Robert's Point: 600m

OBSCUR-O-METER

The Robert's Point track is the ONLY day-walking track, at either FJ or Fox Glacier, which delivers you to a viewpoint above the ice fields. Robert's Pt itself is a rock knob about 400m above the valley floor, directly across from 800m waterfall stair-stepping its wispy way down to the ice field. The track is rough, rocky and steep—superb for fit trampers in fine weather, but maybe best to avoid it in wet weather. The track itself packs plenty of interests, including heaps of swingbridges and the century-old Hendes Hut (look for 1913 signatures on the hut's tin walls!) Additionally, just past the hut is one of most unique track-engineering feats on the South Island. This so-called "Hendes Galley" is a 50-meter steep, suspended planked semi-stairway bolted against the cliff face high above the valley floor— definitely no place for those with fear of heights! 100 years ago you went down this galley-way directly onto the glacier, but now the glacier has retreated another 2km up the valley.

Reaching Robert's Pt you'll find a picnic table and a somewhat obscured view directly down onto the glacial face—a view only the helicopters otherwise get. All the jagged glory of Franz Josef Glacier wrinkles below in white-blue-black majesty. If you want an even better view for all the effort it took to reach this point, then be sure to pick your way down a bit

from the picnic table and then to the right where you'll finally come out onto an open rock slope that sports excellent down-valley views all the way to Lake Mapourika and the Tasman Sea—wow! You'll also see heaps of glacier-walkers marching like ants on the ice field below... and of course the view across the glacier to the stupendous waterfall is unmatched. If you want a strenuous tramp in the glaciers region that delivers good bang-for-the-buck and gets you away from the tourist mob, then Robert's Pt it is!!

Belgian girls at Robert's Point

FJ ice-walkers

Tramp Expect a strenuous true tramping track with lots of wet roots, rocks, and swing-bridges. The track is marked the entire way with no junctions or options. It's 10 min to the first bridge, then 20 more drops you back to the valley floor via steps. Now the real climbing begins...20 minutes to Hendes Hut, then a non-stop 50-minute ascent to the Point. All along the way there are plenty of stream-crossing splash spots.

West Coast-SOUTH

Hendes Galley

DRIVING: Head up the FJ Glacier Valley road. You can begin at the road-end carpark, but doing so adds an extra dullish 1.0km. The better start point is 1km before the glacier road-end at the Lake Wombat trailhead. Across from the Wombat track you'll see a track that quickly leads to the DOC sign announcing the track.

D9 ▶ FOX GLACIER VALLEY TRACK

CROWDED ROUTE TO THE SNOUT

Walk: easy 17-minute (1.5km) one-way

- watch YouTube: bhkLvijcoga & pnqg3yj2iLk
- bring: plastic bag, hammer

OBSCUR-O-METER

Fox Glacier track

West Coast· SOUTH

The easy viewpoint walk to Fox Glacier's snout only takes half the time and effort as the walk to Franz Josef, and thus EVERY tour bus and EVERY tourist chooses this walk if they only have time for one glacier walk. Expect LARGE walking groups. Even though it can seem fairly crowded, everyone should do it, even if you've already walked up FJ's valley. Fox's ice-wall snout is more impressive than FJ's...more crevassed and buckled and less covered with dirt and debris than Franz's, showing more of that wonderful glacial blue between all the black streaking.

The walk is short, and since you can't see as high up the valley from where the track is, the actual walk is less captivating than FJ's. To liven the walk up a bit bring a plastic grocery sack and take note of the gravel-covered block of "dead ice" oozing water just 100m into the track from the carpark. On the way back from the ice wall take a step up the "dead ice" and give

Fox viewpoint

the edges a knock to chip off your own handful of dirty glacial ice. This big hunk of glacial ice has been sitting there melting for 50 years—since the glacier's retreat up the valley in the 1960s! Chip off some hunks, give 'em a rinse, and then either have a mouthful of glacier or use them to glacier-chill a cocktail!

Dead Ice

DRIVING: 2km south of Fox Glacier town turn onto the glacier-access road on the north side of the bridge.

AN ELEVATED VIEW OF FOX GLACIER'S UPPER REACHES

Walk: moderate 30-minute (2km) one-way

● elevation carpark: 260m
● elevation viewpoint: 440m

OBSCURE · POPULAR
OBSCUR-O-METER

The Chalet track is a moderately uphill track ending at a view platform overlooking Fox Glacier's blue-black icy snout. This is an impressive glacial view for a relatively paltry effort…and better yet, no tour buses bring their hordes up here. The Chalet track is fine-weather-only,as drizzle makes it slippery and lots of rain makes a stream-crossing impassable. On a sunny day, this track, more than any other FJ/Fox Glacier track, highlights the unique nature of these NZ glaciers—alpine ice mixed with rainforest. On the way to the historic "chalet" view you'll think you're in the tropics as tree ferns hung with moss line the track,

Chalet view

epiphytic plants hang from tree limbs, and the summertime red blossoms of the Southern Rata trees are reminiscent of tropical Hibiscus.

Note upper glacier

Fox roadside photo-op

Arriving at the track's-end viewpoint, you'll find one of the few locations in the world where you can frame both ferns and glacier in the same photo—neat! Looking closely at the upper glacier you'll undoubtedly see the ant-like ice-walkers, and below to the left is the Fox Glacier valley-walk viewpoint. Surrounding the viewpoint the Southern Alps ridgelines tower 1,200 meters above you!

FYI ► The better view of the complete top-to-bottom Fox Glacier is from the roadside signed viewpoint, not the steep 15-min track to the disappointingly overgrown "Fox Glacier viewpoint".

DRIVING: South of Fox Glacier town, turn onto the glacier access road on the <u>south</u> side of the Fox River bridge, then 3km to the road-end carpark.

West Coast - SOUTH

D11 ▶ FOX GLACIER'S LAKE MATHESON

FAMOUS ALPS—REFLECTION PHOTO—OP

Walk: easy one-hour (4km) loop walk

● watch YouTube: 65Lvfp5bo-u

OBSCURE POPULAR
OBSCUR-O-METER

The early morning reflection of Mts Tasman and Cook in the still tannin-stained waters of Lake Matheson is as perfect as a reflection photo gets. Wonderfully, DOC has extended the "Reflection Island" viewpoint steps right down to the lakeside point where the reflection shines best. Expect plenty of tourist company on this lakeshore loop because every tour bus stops here and the easy walk over to the lake makes the outing all-ages friendly. The track makes a loop around the entire lake with stops at two viewpoint platforms (Reflection Island is the better one.)

Tasman   Cook

Reflection Island view

For keen photographers, neither dawn nor sunset is best for lighting the reflection scene. Dawn is WAY too back-lit and near dusk the entire Fox Glacier canyon is in deep shadow. In the afternoon, when the light may be best, that's when the glacier breeze stirs up the lake. Thus, the time that the photo-pros go to get their "shot" would be mid-morning on a calm sunny day—about 8:30-9am (of course on a clear calm sunny day...Ha!) This lets the rising sun creep high enough to light some of the foreground ridges, but before the thermal winds begin to blow. As a photographer, don't bother to sleep in the carpark and hustle out at dawn, because dawn only disappoints. Wait for the tourist airplanes to begin their daily rumble, have a nice brekkie at the Lake café, then go. Regrettably, this is when the daily tour buses begin arriving. Best of luck—it is a smashing photo when the elements are kind.

Eel!

From the Reflection Island photo platform be sure to look for the "friendly" eel family that lives under the platform. Every now and then one or more may swim out from under the platform to check-out the daily human parade... yikes!

Walk An easy one-hour track (4km) circles the lake. Going clockwise, the small, cramped "View of Views" platform is about 25 minutes, then 8 more minutes to Reflection Island. To speed your way to

Mt. Cook
Peak Viewpoint
Past the lake

Reflection Island, begin the track then turn right to go counter-clockwise.

FYI There's another great photo-op "Peak Viewpoint" another 5km past the Lake Matheson turn, on the way to Gillespies Beach at the stream crossing—check it out, as it lets you see the upper Fox Glacier.

Fox Glacier   Mt. Tasman   Mt. Cook
"Peak Viewpoint" area

DRIVING: From Fox Glacier town take the signed road 4km to the signed Lake Matheson turn.

113

HELLO/GOODBYE WEST COAST!!

Walk: Roadside beach sculptures

● watch YouTube: _avzcupe–re

OBSCURE · POPULAR

OBSCUR-O-METER

West Coast · SOUTH

This section of the West Coast highway runs right along the beach for a couple km, and if you're traveling southwards, this is the first time the highway has hugged the shoreline since Punakaiki. For some reason travelers stop along this section of coastline every year to stack rocks into some peculiar balancey combinations. Who knows why?? Because it's the final glimpse of the Tasman for southbound travelers? Because it's the first glimpse for northbounders? Call it whimsy, joy, love......whatever it is, people stop and create traveler tributes to NZ every year. Always the same, but always different.

Where's yours?

DRIVING: 45km south of Fox Glacier, or 25km north of Lake Paringa.

114

D13 > MONRO BEACH TRACK

A BEACH WITH RARE PENGUINS

Walk: easy 30-minute (2.5km) one-way to beach

• watch YouTube: 6s2y_ff4abo & 7fk3-oohckw

OBSCUR-O-METER

Monro Beach is probably your best chance to spot an elusive Fiordland Crested Penguin, as well as taking a peaceful jungle walk to a sandy beach cove. Numerous signs at the beach and trailhead describe the rare and poorly-understood penguins. Unlike the Yellow-Eyed penguins, the FC penguins go to sea for months at a time without returning to their nests. The best time to see the FCPs is July-December when they come ashore to breed, and then again in Jan-Feb when they come ashore again to moult. (I've seen one, and

O B S E R V E

C O N S E R V E

feel lucky. On Jan 30, 2010 at 3:30pm it popped ashore and waddled up the beach and then quickly hopped up the brushy slope to its nest.)

Monro Beach

Regardless of whether you'll see a penguin, the easy 30-minute walk to the beach cove is very pleasant. It's a nearly-flat walking tour through a dense Westland jungle of fern, moss, Rata and Kahikatea with birdsong and stream gurgle accompanying your steps. A very nice easy walk!

West Coast–SOUTH

A low-tide is the best time to visit Monro Beach. First, because a lower tide gives the penguins farther to walk up the sand to get to the bush (and thus more chance to see them). Second, about two hours either side of low tide you can sneak around the headland cliffs to

explore longer beaches either north or south. Head north on the wild beach for 20 minutes (1.3km) and you may find a clear-water lagoon where the next stream enters the beach. Head south for 10 minutes to see the stream that empties Lake Moeraki.

Monro Beach

North beach lagoon

DRIVING: The signed beach track is on SH 6 at the western end of Moeraki Lake, near the Lodge. It's about 30km north of Haast or 19km south of Lake Paringa.

RIVERS AND WATERFALLS

Drive: 90 km from Sea to Lake Wanaka

• watch YouTube: rngwLLgL7bg & m9czruu_t5y

OBSCUR-O-METER

Haast Pass is the most southern, the rainiest, and the lowest of the three passes. Haast is the ethereal rainforest and waterfalls pass compared to Arthur's alpine grandeur and Lewis's hot springs. The 90km journey over Haast Pass from Tasman Sea to Lake Wanaka (or vice versa) features plenty of quick bang-for-the-buck stops, but no substantial walking tracks or all-day interest points. Most travelers hustle the Haast, eager to either get to Wanaka...or get to the coast. There are a few DOC camps along the route for people who want to break up the Haast Pass drive. Otherwise, waterfalls and river/mountain views will greet you around every corner of the drive.

Here's a km-by-km run-down of some of the Haast stopping-point attractions, beginning on the west coast at Haast Township (not the VisCtr) (0km). 22km to Depot Creek Falls...27km to Roaring Billy Falls...47km to Pleasant Flats DOC camp...51km to Thunder Creek Falls...57km to Fantail Falls...61km to Haast Pass...71km to Blue Pools...80km to Makaroa town...90km to Lake Wanaka.

Depot Creek Falls. This 35m-ish falls is one of the Haast's secrets. There's no sign on the road, but there is a gravel carpark immediately east of the signed Depot Creek bridge. From the parking a wee path leads one minute to the secretive waterfall. It's the "secret" nature of this spot that makes it special, not because the waterfall is overly special. Pretty much guaranteed solitude. Maybe climb up a bit and have a splash in the couple-sized pool with your partner and share a smile that none of the rushing Haast tourists even know you and this waterfall are hiding in the forest.

Depot Creek Falls

Drive: 22km east of Haast Township (1.0km past the signed Cache Creek bridge), or 5km west of Roaring Billy.

Roaring Billy Falls. Roaring Billy is a good stop for a short little walk, especially if you're coming from the east and have just spent time on the island's dry side. The flat 5-minute track to Roaring Billy's view is a wonderful re-introduction to the wet West Coast jungle. Palms and hanging moss everywhere, dense impenetrable bush, and even a big tree that you can stand inside of. On the other hand, if you've just come down the wet coast, you're probably sick of jungle and can't wait for Wanaka's sunshine...so skip this. Once down the track you get a distant view of the so-so falls (most impressive after mega-rain), but if you descend to the shingle riverbed and walk over, the Haast River shows an alluring opaque blue as it quietly glides by the Roaring Billy.

Drive: 27km from Haast or 20km west of Pleasant Flats. There's a signed turn-around carpark.

Thunder Creek Falls

Thunder Creek Falls. This is the tour-bus favorite. One minute stop, take picture, hurry on the way. Signs say 28m, but it's quite obviously a good bit higher—more like 40m. No place to explore or play much, just a photo-op.

Drive: 5km east of Pleasants Flats or 10km west of the pass, obviously signed.

Fantail Falls. Fantail Falls has a secret. Walk the 1-minute track to view the falls across the still-young and crystalline Haast River....and you'll think, "What's the secret...this seems just a quick photo-stop?" Fantail Falls itself is simply a picturesque stair-step waterfall pouring into the Haast River...and if it hasn't rained too much you may be able to scramble a bit up the left side of the falls for fun or photo angles.

But Fantail's secret is downstream 200 meters. You may have seen it from the road if you came from the west. Fantail's neighbor stream charges out of a gushing slot canyon. Simply walk down the shingle bed from Fantail and then up the stream pouring from within the jungle. In a minute you'll see that "mist-belching waterfall chasm" sums up the scene pretty well. The only way to get close is to wade through the bottom pool and then scamper up and over the rocks. In fair weather the bottom pool is chest deep, but if you grapple along the left side you can make it through. Fantail's secret provides a good exciting little adventure for gung-ho travelers tired of Haast's tourist photo-ops. Water sandals and swimsuit are the call here.

Fantail Falls

Drive: Fantail is clearly signed 6km east of Thunder Creek or just 3.5km west of the Pass.

Blue Pools. The Blue Pools is a short walk over a fun swingbridge to a fenced viewpoint overlooking a deep blue crystal clear river section. The Blue is akin to Hokitika Gorge (D1),but this Blue is clear rather than opaque. Simply eye-candy yummy on a sunny day!

Drive: 10km east of the Pass or 9km west of Makaroa.

MAPS ON FLICKR!!!

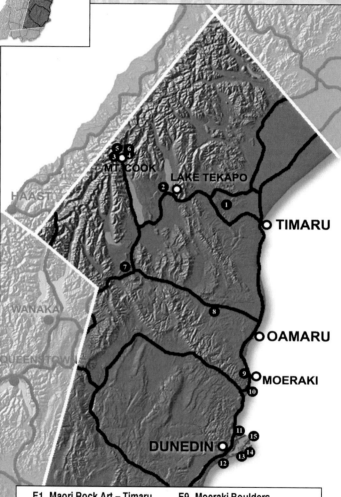

E1 Maori Rock Art – Timaru	E9 Moeraki Boulders
E2 Lake Tekapo	E10 Shag Point
E3 Lake Pukaki/Mt Cook	E11 Mapoutahi Heads/Dr. Pt.
E4 Tasman Glacier Tracks	E12 Tunnel Beach
E5 Hooker Valley Track	E13 Sandfly Bay
E6 Ball Flats Rd Route	E14 Sandymount Track
E7 Clay Cliffs of Omarama	E15 Taiaroa Head/Albatross Ctr.
E8 Duntroon	

SOUTHEAST - LAKES & COAST

The region south of Christchurch down to Dunedin, including the famous lakes Pukaki and Tekapo, is referred to as the MacKenzie Country and Central Otago. The MacKenzie Country is mind-bogglingly gorgeous, the obvious highlights being the two ultra-blue lakes with the snowy peaks of Mt Cook/Southern Alps as the backdrop. Both Lake Pukaki and Lake Tekapo are

must-sees. You'll get a big eye full of Lake Pukaki as you drive alongside it on the way to Mt Cook Village. Lake Tekapo is easily gawked-at from the village shoreline, but much better is to drive/walk up to the Mt John Observatory for a brilliant 360° birds-eye view that will make your shutter-finger ache. These are NZ photos that the folks at home will "oooh and ahhh" over!

Another highlight of the region is its scattering of almost-unknown Maori Rock Art inland from Timaru. All the rock art overhangs/caves have been protected by the Gov't with fencing. The numerous sites are well-known to scholars, but virtually unknown to both Kiwis and travelers.

Down the coast towards Oamaru and Dunedin you'll enter the penguin and Sea lion zone. The rare Yellow-eyed Penguins exclusively nest on the SE coast of NZ, roughly from Oamaru down through the Catlins. The penguins are amazing to watch—see Appendix 2 for more info. See Appendix 3 for Sea lion/seal info.

Dunedin is the South Island's second biggest city and very worthy of a look (In my opinion Dunedin is a more interesting city to visit than Chch). Dunedin has a lively university-town feel, interesting Scottish architecture/heritage, and plenty of outdoor attractions. The Otago Peninsula, angling into the Pacific from Dunedin, is similar to Chch's Banks Peninsula in that it is the flooded remnants of a one-time volcano. The drive on the Otago Peninsula is outstanding! In town, on a grey day, don't miss the excellent free Otago Museum and its Southern Lands exhibit. St Clair beach has heated salt water pools. Possibly worth a look is "The world's steepest street" in north Dunedin (bring your zorb).

Don't miss:
  Tekapo/Pukaki/Mt Cook (2-6)
  Moeraki's penguins (9)
  Taniwha Rock Art (1)
  Otago Peninsula (13-15)

E1 MAORI ROCK ART DRAWINGS– TIMARU AREA

BEST CONCENTRATION OF ROCK PAINTINGS ON SOUTH ISLAND

Walk: various short scramble explorations

• bring: i-Site area map, call ahead to Opihi Vineyard

OBSCUR-O-METER

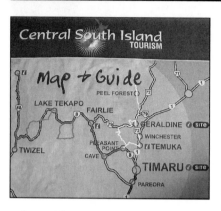

The Timaru area hosts NZ's most interesting collection of Maori rock art sites, but most of these sites remain unknown to travelers, as well as most area locals. All these rock art sites are protected with extensive fencing, so it's not as if nobody knows the art is there. If you are at all interested in pictographs and such, then spend an afternoon chasing down these elusive sites. You'll see a "real" NZ that few know exists. 100% pure off-the-beaten-path, to say the least!

A Maori Rock Art center is planned near the Timaru i-Site, but as of yet, nothing. If you want to attempt to find these obscure and scattered rock art sites, it's imperative to check in with either the Timaru or Geraldine i-Site. These i-Sites stock a free "Central South Island Tourism" map with the rock art sites located with icons and the detailed street name/locations to find your way to the sites. I'll attempt to give some directions here, but be fore-warned, if you only have a KiwiMaps or a Hema Maps, neither is detailed enough to find the obscure spots.

Frenchman's Gully "Te Manunui" site. This site has some small but amazingly detailed drawings. Also, it has a fabulous interpretive display panel that details heaps of info about the drawings, the area, and the nature and interpretation of the rock art. The drawings in the entire area have sometimes been "improved" with scratched out-lines—apparently an attempt by early scientists to "help" visualize the drawings.

DRIVE: Signs on the road point the way to this developed site, but only once you're within the final 1.3km. The site is off of Pareora River Rd, which runs between Cave and Pareora, a bit SW of Timaru. From SH 1, take Pareora Rd about 12km NW towards Cave. Cross a river ford, stay left at the fork and go 4km more to Craigmore Valley

120

Rd. Go left onto Craig-more for 2.5km then left at the sign for rock art and 1.3km more to the signed site. (Craigmore Vly Rd is about 18km south of Cave).

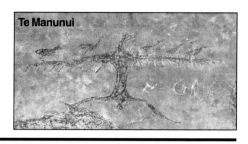

Te Manunui

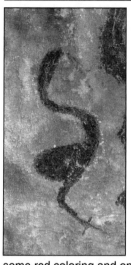

Hazelburn-Blacklers Cave. This area, all on private farmlands, has 3 different sites to view, all within 700 meters. The first is the furthest in and it has an excellent Taniwha (demon) as well as a nice waka (war canoe). This site is unmarked. You park on the road shoulder, hop over a stile, and clamber up a steep 30m hill to the rock art overhang.

To find the parking spot, pass the long grey metal barn on the right, and **just 25m past it**, on the left, look for the easy-to-miss path heading up and left to a stile with limestone cliffs above.

The 2nd/3rd two sites are back on the paved road before the barns. About 200m before the end of the pavement there's a faint path on the south side leading a quick 6m to a fenced overhang site. Not too much to see here, but some red coloring and one Big Bird!

The third site is the most difficult to get to, but also one of the best rock art sites on the entire island! Back a few meters on the road from site 2, across the paddock and up the hill is a limestone gully with a big wide tree at its base and a powerline up and right. There's a stile to get across the fence here. The rock art is a steep 40m climb up the gully, but first you've got to cross the boggy stream at the base of the tree. There's no easy way here mate, you've got to earn these pictographs!

3rd site cave

Stream

Stile

121

cont'd ➡

Either splash across the stream or possibly get a dry assist from the overhanging tree (I was able to cross dry-footed). Zig-zag your way up the gully and look for the fenced overhang. Wow, fabulous drawings of men, demons, and even meres (war clubs).

DRIVE: This site is tricky to find, impossible without the local map. It's NW of Pleasant Point/Cave. From either of those villages take Totara Valley Rd/ Cleland Rd (Cleland Rd is 3.5km east of Cave.) At the northern arc of Totara Valley Rd (about 12km from either direction) turn onto Raincliff Rd and in 1km go left onto Monument Rd. Go 4 km then left at Three Mile Bush Rd. The three sites are on this road. Go 1km until the end of pavement—the first site is 500m ahead on the gravel, the 2nd/3rd are 200m behind.

<u>Raincliff DOC site.</u> This is the most developed/signed site and the easiest to find...but the worst to view. There's very little to see except smudges...but the smudges are well-signed and protected. The site is approx 10km south of SH 79 on Gudex Rd, or 4.7 km north of the previous rock art site. The signed site on Raincliff/Middle Vly Rd is just north of the Scout Camp/river bridge crossing.

<u>Opihi Vineyard site.</u> Surprisingly, this site's not on the free map...but it's special. **So special that the painting here has its own name—"Taniwha", which was once featured on a 1960s NZ postage stamp. This is the best rock art in NZ. (Say Tan-ifa.)**

Access is through the property of Opihi Vineyards. The vineyard's café is an excellent place to lunch in the middle of a day of rock art exploring, toasting your findings with a glass of wine, coffee, or eats. To find the rock art you need to pop into the café and ask the owner, Allan, for his directions map (without his map you'll never find the site, as it's on his homestead property). **This means you need to visit when the café is OPEN! (roughly Weds-Sunday, 11am-4pm)** Allan is as gracious as a Kiwi comes and he'll gladly describe the tricky route to find Taniwha, and then he'll give you a copy of his treasure map and send you on the 1.5km drive and 5-minute walk to the site. Check www.opihi.co.nz. Address is 804 Opihi Rd, Opihi, Pleasant Pt. Phone 64 3 614 8308

(Here's a personal anecdote: I've photographed petroglyphs all over the USA and Mexico, and let me tell you that Taniwha is special. SO special that I won't tell you more. Go see for yourself—it's not hard to see, given it's more than 6 meters long! And, for photos …don't snap from behind the fencing, as the angle will distort. Reach your camera through, aim

Viewing Taniwha

at the same incline as Taniwha…and crop later. Sit with Taniwha and let your eyes adjust to the light and ceiling contours…the glyphs get better as your eyes adapt. This is as impressive of a rock art design as I've ever seen anywhere…yet here it hides in the hinterlands of Timaru as one of the island's best-kept secrets. Please check my Flickr/blog for bigger photos.)

2/-

MAORI ROCK DRAWING
NEW ZEALAND

DRIVE: From the Raincliff site go back south 5.5km, turn left on Totara Valley Rd then immediately left onto Gays Pass Rd for 3km over to the Opihi Vineyard. Or, from Pleasant Point take Opihi Valley Rd about 10km to vineyard. Opihi Vineyard is just south of Hanging Rock.

Note to readers: please let me know if this info was enough to get you to these spots...and if it was worth it. NZfrenzy@yahoo.com

Complete Taniwha drawing (from rock art book)

2 meter section of Taniwha!

E2 ▶ **LAKE TEKAPO**
(teeka-poe)

GORGEOUS BLUE. GORGEOUS VIEW!!

Walk: moderate 30-minute (2.5 km) one-way

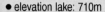

- elevation lake: 710m
- watch YouTube: h19zs–vzazy & shiazb81bvk

OBSCUR-O-METER

Lake Tekapo's aquamarine blue color is simply beyond description. On a sunny day it's jaw-drop, eye-boggling beautiful. **You NEED to see it!** On a grey day the beauty dims, but the blue opacity of the lake water still impresses. Lake Tekapo is the postcard-perfect fabled beauty of New Zealand.

There's not much for travelers to do at Lake Tekapo other than just stare at the lake and take yet another photo, but there are a few options. The lake is glacier-cold year-round, so don't plan on swimming. Mostly just plan for a laid-back day of relaxing eye-candy.

Lake Tekapo Village. Hosts a number of restaurants, each with a killer lake view. Tourists and tour buses crowd to the nearby and uber-scenic "Church of the Good Shepherd" for the obligatory photo-ops. The church features what may be the picturesque chapel-view on the planet, with the bonus of having the iconic sheep-herding dog sculpture just a 100m walk away. As an extra, pop inside the Godley Hotel to see some 1950s photos of the church.

Lakeside Church of the Good Shepherd

Mt John Observatory. This celestial observatory, some 300m above the town atop 1,031m Mt John, is a MUST-SEE! The 360° view from the Mt John's Astro Café is beyond fabulous! Of course the view over Lake Tekapo to the distant snow-capped peaks steals the show, but on a sunny day look for the peak of Mt. Cook/Aoraki poking over the western ridgeline. Notice too that Tekapo's neighbor lake, Lake Alexandrina, makes for an

Mt. John's Astro Café

interesting color contrast—both lake formed in the same glacier-gouged manner, but since Alexandrina doesn't receive any direct glacial stream flow, it receives none of the "rock flour" that colors Tekapo, leaving it just a regular blue.

Looking south over town you'll see the now-dry riverbed and the snaking hydro canal that steals the river flow. Imagine the beauty of the former ribbon of aqua blue flowing through the sparse desert. Locals report that the blue river does sometimes actually still flow due to rain and run-off, usually about once a month.

There are two ways to get up to Mt John. The easy way is via an 8km drive from the village, the last 3km fairly steep but still paved (In my opinion this is one the finest drive-to viewpoints on the island, challenged by only Q-town/Wanaka's ski-resort roads).

Or, for walkers a moderate track starts at mapboard carpark near the Alpine Spa. For the fit it's 30-min up, with the option to make a longer 2-hour loop. The track is well-graded as it climbs the 300m to the peak, with better Lake Tekapo views unfolding the entire way up, until, WOW, the view at the café knocks your socks off!!

Alpine Spring Spa. This new-ish spa resort/park is a delight. The resort features 3 large pools of heated spring water, all overlooking the blueblue lake and surrounding mountains. Hanmer Springs must be jealous of this setting! The three pools are charmingly named, shaped, and tiered like the 3 area lakes—Ohau, Pukaki, and Tekapo. The sunset view is divine. Open from 10am to 10pm, about $16-$20pp.

YouTube vid:
4r7pzv09ksc

Alpine Spring Spa

125

"GOD'S COUNTRY" BEAUTY!!

Walk: various walks
- elevation village: 750m
- watch YouTube: n–L8Lrx–u7y
- bring: sunny weather

OBSCUR-O-METER

The 55km drive along the western shore of gorgeous opaque-blue Lake Pukaki towards Mt Cook Village is one of the most enjoyable sunny-day drives on the island. It's the kind of picturesque scene that adorns many a guidebook cover and postcard rack. Every km brings you a little closer to Mt Cook's jagged crest dominating the skyline ahead, while every corner of the road showcases another view down over the sweeping expanse of Pukaki's unreal blue-ness. This drive is 100% pure NZ pleasure! Interesting to note is that when you're in the Village, you are now closer to the Tasman Sea (40km) than you are to the far end of Lake Pukaki.

Arriving at Mt Cook Village you'll find an epic sweeping alpine vista at every turn of your head. You're only problem will be choosing which of the many walking options to venture onto first. Here are some in-sights, as everything depends on the cloud

Mt. Cook

Lake Pukaki

cover. It's best to plan at least 2-3 days in the Village area to give you the chance to see the snow-capped peaks and glaciers in glorious sunshine. If Mt Cook is clouded-over, then bide your time and save the Hooker Valley walk and its Mt Cook views for a clearer day. Viewing the Tasman Glacier, doing the iceberg-boat tour, or walking some portion of the Ball Flats route are all good cloudy-weather options. When the sun shines, maybe climb to Red Tarn in the morning when you're energized, then go up the easier Hooker Valley mid-day.

Tracks The Hooker Valley walk tops the must-see list. The track to Kea Pt is also super-worth it for a shorter outing (2km one-way, 170m elevation gain). The two "tarn" tracks—Sealy and Red—are both view-packed as well, but both require steep ascents for their visual splendors. Sealy Tarns spurs off the Kea Pt track and climbs about 600 vertical meters to the above-treeline reflective tarns where you'll get a birds-eye view of two glacial lakes, the entire Hooker Valley and gargantuan Mt Cook. The Red Tarn track is south of the Village and climbs about 300 vertical meters to a sweeping view encompassing the Village as well as the Mueller Glacier lake and Mt Cook.

SHORT TRACKS TO ICEBERG VIEWS

**Walk: Easy and moderate short walks
(500m to 1.3km one-way)**

• watch YouTube: w6ddrvb2ptq & 5c5j1ieutzc

OBSCUR-O-METER

Glacier View Track: A Must-See! The 15-minute steep stepped-track to the top of the Tasman Glacier's moraine ridge is amazing. The track is Steep, but the payoff is worth it! The view sweeps over the entire glacial lake and its scattered flotilla of icebergs. This birds-eye view down onto the glacial toe and lake is quite unlike any on the Hooker Valley/Lake track. The Tasman Glacier itself hardly looks like a glacier, given that it's covered

Tasman Glacier

Ball Flats Route

Glacier Lake

Tasman Glacier Viewpoint

with a heap of black rubble with only small slices of white showing up through its rubble covering. Looking up the glacier to the 3,000m+ peaks at its head—Mts Tasman and Haast—it's interesting to ponder that these are the very peaks that also spawn the both the Franz Josef and Fox Glaciers that flow westward. Both West Coast glacier valleys are no more than 30km from this very viewpoint!

From the Tasman Glacier view the commercial iceberg-tour boats can often be seen below cruising amongst the 'bergs. These boats, surprisingly named "Titanic" and "Global Warmer"*, give you a good perspective how mammoth those icebergs are! (*just kidding about the names.)

Tasman Lake Track: It's about an easy 15-minute one-way (1.3km) walk to a lake-level view of the lake and its turbid outlet river. This view isn't nearly as interesting as the "glacier view" from atop the moraine ridge. This track is the access point for the iceberg-view boat dock.

Blue Lakes Track: These two impounded glacial tarn-lakes are hardly worth the quick look, as they are not as blue as they once were.

Iceberg-tour boat

SE Lakes & Coast

DRIVING: Just before arriving at Mt Cook Village turn at the signed "Tasman Valley" junction and take the gravel road a washboardy 7.5km to the road-end carpark.

E5 ▸ HOOKER VALLEY TRACK

SOUTH ISLAND'S BEST DAY—WALK

Walk: moderate 70-minute (5 km) one-way
- elevation carpark: 750m
- elevation lake: 860m
- watch YouTube: arsiL8sidp8

OBSCURE POPULAR
OBSCUR-O-METER

On a clear day, the Hooker Valley Track is indisputably the South Island's most scenic day walk. <u>Indisputably!!</u> On a grey clouded-in day, forget it. This walk is all about soaring alpine views, so if the clouds are socked-in and low, wait for another day (the Ball Flat Route is a better clouded-day option).

On a clear morning even the carpark dazzles with one of the most scenic settings on the island, and from there the excursion just gets better— WAY better! You'll witness huge glaciers oozing down jagged ridges, waterfalls spewing from blue-tinged hanging glaciers, moraine-dammed glacial lakes with floating icebergs, chocolate-brown rivers, wispy waterfalls...all capped by Aoraki's towering presence. Quite a track!!

Mt. Cook/Hooker Glacier

Mueller Lake

Hooker Valley

A few steps into the track you'll arrive at a perfect viewpoint over the glacial latte-brown Lake Mueller spilling its coffee-colored river under an oh-so-scenic swingbridge. Continuing, you'll soon cross a second swingbridge over the Hooker Gorge—a bouncy fun bridge spanning scenery to die for. Then the track gets better and even more scenic as you turn a corner and Aoraki literally pierces the clouds in the valley ahead— an arresting sight! From there, the last half of the track to Hooker's glacier moraine lake at the base of Aoraki just gets better and better as the oooohs and ahhhhs pile up. Innumerable waterfalls tumble, the coffee river roars,

SE Lakes & Coast

Approaching Aoraki

and the sight of Aoraki defies description. The track underfoot is fun in and of itself as it alternates rock-hopping and planked tussock boardwalks. At the final bend of the track a last surprise awaits as Hooker Lake pops into view...from its iceberg-pocked shore to its calving glacial snout, all with 3,754m Aoraki reigning above. Wow.

This track is deservedly popular, so expect mid-day crowds. If you want to shed the crowd of picnickers on the rocks at the first sight of the lake, then simply boulder-hop your way along the shoreline. If you de-shoe and cross the first stream you'll leave 97% of the normal folk behind...and if you keep rock-hopping along the shoreline another 20 minutes, not only do you leave 100% behind, but you'll also get an increasingly better view of the twin 600m waterfalls spilling from the east-side ridge and a better close-up of the glacial snout. Keep an eye on the

3,754m Aoraki
Hooker Glacier
860m Hooker Lake

glacier—if you see it calve a huge chunk into a massive splash, you'll be glad you made the extra effort to be close. How many other places feature calving glaciers, cloud-piercing peaks, and thousand-foot waterfalls all in a glance?? Gotta love 100% Pure New Zealand, Aoraki style!

DRIVING: Immediately before Mt Cook Village turn at the signs for Hooker Valley and go 2km to the road-end carpark.

SE Lakes & Coast

E6 ▶ BALL FLATS ROAD ROUTE

OFF-THE-BEATEN-TRACK ALONG TASMAN GLACIER

Walk/Tramp: moderate 1 to 2-hour one-way (6 to 9km)

- elevation: carpark – 730 m / Ball Flats – 1030 m
- bring: warm jacket

OBSCUR-O-METER

A high-clearance 4WD road follows the western edge of the Tasman Glacier moraine ridge about two-thirds the way to the former site of the historic Ball Hut. This road route begins at the Tasman Glacier-view carpark. This road, built just after World War 1, accessed the once-popular Ball Hut/skifields. Incredibly, given the current rough-4WD condition of the road, it's hard to imagine that buses of skiers once used to drive the 9km up to the Ball Hut.

Rock-covered Tasman Glacier

Ball Route

Nowadays the 4WD road—the 6km that still exists—makes an excellent day-walk. If walking up a road on the viewless side of a moraine ridge doesn't sound too exciting (it originally didn't sound too exciting to me), just wait…this route is impressive, and you'll probably only see a handful of people all day!

Beginning the route you'll first amble beside a rushing blue stream… then there are various access points up the 25m moraine ridge for peeks down at the glacier lake and icebergs…and all the while there are mountains all around with canyon clefts filled with waterfalls cascading into mini-glacier ice caves. Oh yeah, and at the end of the road you've got an amazing panorama of the white portion of the Tasman Glacier uppers rounding a corner before becoming a blackened and rubble-covered Mordor-like slag. Quite impressive indeed! Once you reach the end of the 4WD road, there's a marked DOC route to the former site of the now-removed Ball Hut. This

Looking back from Ball Flats

Tourist
Viewpoint Carpark

Ball
Flats

section past the road-end becomes very rough, mostly over rock and rubble. Given that the historic Ball Hut is no longer there, and they view isn't too much better at the hut site than at the end of the 4WD road, it may be best to just turn back at the road-end unless you've got heaps of time and energy.

If you're keen to explore the mini-glacier waterfall and ice cave, bring a warm coat because the cave is drippy and freezing cold. And, stay off the middle of the mini-glaciers—just walk the edges. The middle of these snow fields are very thin and prone to collapse.

Route ▶ Walking from the Glacier-view carpark it's an easy 70 minutes to the 4WD road-end (6km) and then an optional rough-going 50 minutes more (3km) to the former Ball Hut site. Elevation gain is 300m to Ball Flats.

From the glacier-view carpark the first 2km follows the Blue Stream up to the signed "Avalanche Area." As you approach the high point of the road over the avalanche debris, notice that the blue stream disappears! Check downhill of the sign to see the stream "springing-forth". At the road's high point there's a path up the moraine ridge for some non-tourist-choked

lake views. Continuing up the road, in 30 minutes more you'll come to "The Cove" where a waterfall tumbles into a mini yellow-ish glacier. The glacier and waterfall and ice-cave are all cool to explore, but it's best to save them for the route back (in case you get wet). Now walk 20 minutes more until the road ends atop the moraine ridge where boulders and wash-outs block the way. Either turn back here or follow DOC's rugged marked route over the boulder fields another 50-60 minutes to Ball Flats.

Snow Field

Ice Cave

DRIVING: Same as Tasman Glacier view.

SE Lakes & Coast

E7 **CLAY CLIFFS OF OMARAMA**
(O-mara-ma)

ERODED PINNACLE "BADLAND" CLIFFS

Tramp: easy 30-min walk, or scramble
exploration

• watch YouTube: zkocqg37v4y

OBSCUR-O-METER

The Clay Cliffs are a colorfully eroded "badlands" canyon. These unique cliffs are both fascinating and beautiful, but they don't get much traveler publicity because they're on private land. The small eroded area features orange/grey/yellow striped minarets and spires....pillars and slot canyons and archway tunnels...and cathedral-like amphitheaters festooned with purple lupines. The odd Clay Cliffs are wonderfully photogenic, being set against a nice backdrop of scenic mountains and the blue braided Ahuriri River flowing below. If DOC were in possession of the land there'd be publicity, tracks, view platforms and such...but there's none of that here—the Clay Cliffs are for curious explorers willing to make their own exploratory adventure. There are no signs or pointers—you just explore on your own. The

The Cathedral Canyon

gracious land owners allow access for a paltry fee of **$5 per car**. If you like peculiar geology, then these badlands are a must-see 1-2 hour detour.

Walk Most people simply walk 15 minutes to the end of the 4WD track and pop into the "Wow" cathedral for some great pix, a look-around, and maybe a scramble up a bit to a view-spot. If you're keen to explore more you'll find plenty to intrigue you—just go up the sheep paths or any of the gullies. Each gully hides its own magic slot tunnels. Be warned that the brush is a bit prickly here, so wear long pants and long sleeves to explore deeper.

DRIVING: The cliffs are located off of SH 8, 25km south of Twizel or 5km north of Omarama. Turn at the "Clay Cliffs" road sign and go 4km then left onto the signed gravel road for another 3.5km. At the Clay Cliffs gate pay the $5 and drive 3.3km, then through the next gate and 500m more until the road wash-out under the cliffs.

SE Lakes & Coast

E8 ▶ DUNTROON

THE LAND THAT TIME FORGOT

Visit: Vanished World Centre
Walk: various short walks

• watch YouTube: xLgLkshxpqg & e2-mtbfjzqs

OBSCURE — POPULAR
OBSCUR-O-METER

The area surrounding Duntroon has some quick interesting spots to visit, though nothing that is high on any "must-see" list. Duntroon is about a 30-minute drive from Oamaru.

Vanished World Centre is a small museum in "downtown" Duntroon. Gets maps and info about all the local sights and pay about $5 to see the fossil exhibits, weird rocks and Duntroon-ish stuff.

The road from Duntroon to Ngapara:

This road features most of the Duntroon interest-stops. Begin the route (Dansey's Pass Rd) just east of Vanished Ctr and zero your odometer.

First up is the **Maerewhenua Maori rock-art site**, just 1km from Duntroon. Not too many memorable paintings to see, but worth a quick peek.

Elephant Rocks

Then it's 5km more to **Elephant Rocks**, a mini collection of limestone boulders akin to Castle Hill (entry B7). Basically you can walk anywhere you want to explore the clustered-together boulders. Expect to spend 20-30 minutes looking around. Narnia filmed massive scenes at the Elephant Rocks. (Look for the Narnia-set poster in Vanished World).

1.0 km farther is the **Anatini whale fossil site**. A 1-minute walk from the roadside parking delivers you to the in-situ whale-bone fossils. Interesting too is the gully before the fossil which is adorned with a cornucopia of turn-of-the-century signatures and some mysterious steps. If you watch Narnia (about minute 84) you'll see this valley and its distinctive limestone arch.

A few km farther the road drops for a short drive through the short and scenic **Valley of the Whales**.

North of Duntroon:

Just 3km north of Duntroon on SH 83 is the **Takiroa Maori rock art site**. This site has a roadside carpark and heaps of historic-info signage. This is a "showcase" site, but sadly there's not too much of interest—most of the goods are in museums. To see some better rock art sites, check entry E1 near Timaru.

Earthquakes. Don't know...I haven't visited the area.

Takiora Rock Art

SE Lakes & Coast

MOERAKI BOULDERS
(moe-racky)

WORLD-FAMOUSLY _WEIRD_ BEACH SPHERES

Walk: various short walks

- watch YouTube: L1bk4iz0e8w
  & zm1gw2awzLy

OBSCUR-O-METER

Boulders, penguins, lighthouse

The well-publicized Moeraki Boulders are certainly unique. Since they are about the oddest thing you'll find on a beach anywhere in the world, the boulders are worth a stop no matter how tourist-adverse you may be. Expect a crowd—walking up the beach towards the boulders feels a bit like Coromandel's Hot water Beach—a heap of tourists all clustered around a small area on a vast beach. Surprisingly, Moeraki's Beach (Hampden) is about 8km long, but the boulders only inhabit about 100 meters of it! Few people venture any further than the boulders, but a 20-minute walk north is well worth it. Farther along the beach eroded boulder bits artistically litter the sand and the cliff face is actually giving birth to a handful of baby Moerakis. Mid-tide or lower is the best time to see/climb/examine the boulders, and to walk up the beach to find more bits of interest.

Boulder lovers

Moeraki Village (Fleur's)

Mid-tide Moeraki

SE Lakes & Coast

At the Moeraki boulders there's a cliff-top café which features a sunny deck that's a great vantage to get some chips and watch for the daily Hector's dolphins visits.

Penguins and seal as seen from Hide (6pm)

Katiki Point Lighthouse and Penguins. Moeraki Village is signed 1km south of the boulders. Just 1km in turn right for a 5km gravel road to the lighthouse. The main interest at the lighthouse is the Yellow-eyed Penguin "hide" at Hide Bay. A steep path quickly escorts you into the Hide where windows and binoculars overlook a small penguin nesting beach cove. *5-6pm is penguin Happy-Hour.* The penguins go out hunting all day and return at happy hour to pop up onto the rocks, preen and dry off, then hop and waddle up the short beach to their hidden nests. This is one of the best spots to see penguin action on the entire coast, and surprisingly, only a wee percentage of Moeraki's daily hordes know of it. Last time I was there, from 4:30 to 6pm I saw 8 penguins!

There's also a 10-minute track out to the point that's worth it—lots of seals and shags everywhere, and maybe an up-close and personal with a penguin, since the penguins actually walk the tracks here! The Katiki penguins are all descendants of penguins who were cared-for by the dedicated couple who established this colony site. Thus, these penguins matured with people around, as did their offspring, so on and so on…nowadays the penguins actually breed in burrows along the track, and can be seen strolling the paths often in the daylight! Katiki Pt is truly an amazing penguin-riffic spot that few travelers know about!! (At noon one day I saw 7 penguins—an adult on the track, 2 young in nest holes, and 3 fledglings just hanging out).

Moeraki Village. The village is one of NZ's oldest from 1836. There's a wharf, pub, Holiday Park, and the famed Fleur's restaurant. Turn up Haverford Rd at the Holiday Park for a short drive up the Whaler's Lookout, a 150-year memorial viewpoint where a plaque details the village's history.

To investigate an interesting beach cove sprinkled with odd low-tide rocks and neat orange pebble-sand, go past the wharf to the road-end heli-site and walk the Pa path then go up and over the dirt hill (not the stairway to Whaler's Lookout). Careful of seals at the far end of the beach—they'll roar if you surprise them!

SE Lakes & Coast

Baby
Mama
YEPs on Katiki Pt. path

E10 ▶ **SHAG POINT**
(yeax Baby yeax)

MOERAKI'S LITTLE-KNOWN NEIGHBOR

Walk: drive-up viewpoints or 2km tidal-shelf exploration

• bring: tide chart, swimsuit, water shoes

OBSCURE · POPULAR

OBSCUR-O-METER

Fancy a Shag? All traveling couples should make a short detour off the tourist path out to Shag Point for a little…seals, penguins, and…dinosaurs. Yes, dinosaurs! But first, if you see any Wicked vans a rockin'….well, don't go a knockin'…it's just windy here at Shag Point!

Shag Point is a super-interesting bit of coast, but not for the reason most travelers pop out for a quick look. The publicized DOC area at the actual Point overlooks a seal colony and a small beach where a few Yellow-eyed penguins may come ashore in the late afternoons (if you visit near 5pm you might see some penguins hop up the path directly underneath the viewpoint). Also, there's heaps of fur seals around.

Anyhow, the better reason to check-out Shag Pt is to see the incredible **"Dinosaur Eggs"**!! These "eggs" resemble Moeraki's famed boulders and they sit on a tidal shelf along the Shag Pt road. The most fascinating thing about these "Katiki" boulders is that each one contains some sort of fossil bit in its center that the boulder built itself around, layer by layer (like the formation of a pearl around a grain of sand). Unlike at Moeraki, where the boulders sit on the beach, these "Katiki" boulders are imbedded into the tidal shelf with usually half of the sphere sticking-up out of the mudstone shelf. Get this though—inside one of these Katiki boulders was discovered

Katiki boulder embedded in tidal shelf

Low tide!

SE Lakes & Coast

NZ's largest-ever fossil—an 8-meter Plesiosaur. The entire dinosaur skeleton was the "grain of sand" that the huge boulder formed around!! A sign at Shag Point describes this amazing fact...but typical of off-the-beaten-path NZ, it doesn't tell you where either the Katiki boulders or

Otago Museum display (Dunedin)

this fossil are. Here's the facts: in Dunedin, at the Otago Museum's free "Southern Lands" exhibit, the 8m fossil is laid out on display – it's absolutely amazing! (The entire museum display is also fabulous, especially the multi-Moa collection). The other fact is that you can't see any of these "Katiki boulders" from Shag Pt where the interpretive sign is. You need to back-track along the road because the dinosaur-egg tidal shelf is immediately below the row of seaside cottages.

You can only access the boulder shelf at half-tide or lower—at higher tides the shelf is covered by water. Once you find the public pathway down to the tidal bench you'll be amazed at the odd variety of wave-beaten spheres popping out of the mudstone like pimples. Unlike the Moeraki boulders, these spheres form hollows in their centers which fill with sea water when the tide is out. How fun—these hollowed-out boulders form perfect little sun-warmed natural hot tubs! All mermaids and mermen should bring their swimsuits for a dip in the most unique tide pool you'll ever see (suits are a must, as you are directly under the cottages).

To find the boulders: about 1km back from Shag Point, or 1.7km in from SH 1, look for house marked #183—it has a long brown/red fence and a red mailbox. On its west side is a small gate next to a green hedge.

Katiki mermaid pool

(Underwater at high tide)

From here you'll easily see down onto the boulder-strewn tidal platform. The best boulders are scattered to the left over a 2km stretch. The 20-min walk may take you two hours as you'll want to examine every boulder! Careful of lounging Fur seals and make sure to look for the swaying kelp beds too.

DRIVING: On SH 1, Shag Point is 65km north of Dunedin, 9 km north of Palmerston...or 12km south of Moeraki. Shag Point is signed from the highway.

OFF-THE-BEATEN-TRACK WALKING BEACHES

Walk: easy 40-minute (3km) one-way

• check map on Flickr
• bring: tide chart

OBSCUR-O-METER

Mapoutahi Head is the ridge that separates Purakaunui and Blueskin Bays north of Port Chalmers. Three long white sand beaches adorn the north-facing coastline here, with some intimate low-tide coves adding some pizzazz. The white sand beaches sparkle in the sun with the blue waters and green hillsides nicely

contrasting the arcing sands. The headland is evenly divided into three 1km-long sections, each completely different than the others. The eastern third is a simple long stretch of sand backed by wisping grasses with conical Mt Purakaunui and its bay inlet beckoning ahead. The middle section begins up some steps with an optional quick uphill to a scenic Pa point. Once down on the beach—whoa—a dramatic stretch of white backed by 100m cliffs with the Waitati-Osborne railway perched above. At the western end of this section two sea-cave tunnels escort you out onto Blueskin Bay's

Blueskin Bay/
Doctors Point

Arches

SE Lakes & Coast

low-tide-only Doctor's Pt beach stretch. This section follows the bay's outflow stream as far as Doctor's Point Reserve carpark.

A high tide swamps the sea-cave tunnels and most of all the beaches, so try to plan a mid-tide or lower visit. At low tide you could park at Doctor's Point for a fast-paced walk of the 3km total stretch, but if you plan to linger for awhile and don't want to worry over the tides, then it's best to drive further to the Mapoutahi carpark area.

FYI ▶ The more-eastern Long Beach (signed off the Mapoutahi Rd) has a huge dune-locked sea-cave on its NW end that's big enough for all Otago University to party in…and they do—check it out! The rocks near the cave also sport some short rock-climbing routes.

Mt. Purakaunui

Eastern Beach

DRIVING: About 20km north of Dunedin on SH 1 turn right (east) at Waitati then veer left onto the signed road to Port Chalmers. You'll follow this road for about 15km to the Mapoutahi carpark. Zero your odometer. At the first junction (just 200m), the road to the left is the one to Doctor's Pt.

For Mapoutahi stay straight, then at the odd 4-way angled intersection (3.5km) stay straight and up. At the next T-junction (9km) go left at signs for Purakaunui for 3km then left and down to the bay front. The road becomes gravel here—follow it 4km around the bay to the far NW side until the gravel ends at the tree-forest roadside carpark. Park and walk 10 minutes to the beach.

E12 ▸ TUNNEL BEACH

MAN-MADE TUNNEL TO SUPER-SCENIC BEACH COVE

Walk: moderately steep 15-minute (1km)
one-way to tunnel/cove
- elevation carpark: 140m
- watch YouTube: wxh30tmhhxc

OBSCUR-O-METER

Tunnel Beach wave bash!

Tunnel Beach is more than simply a peculiar hand-carved tunnel leading down to a small low-tide-only sandy cove. While the tunnel, commissioned by civic luminary John Cargill in the 1870's to provide his young daughters access to the beach, is certainly intriguing…the main draws of Tunnel Beach are the scenic sandstone cliffs towering over the pounding surf and land-bridge archway that begs a courageous walk-over. Not only are these sandstone cliffs smashing eye-candy, but they're also good ear-candy if the surf if running high and pounding them with booming fountains of spray! The tunnel access to the sandy cove is pretty much a half-tide or lower only, but regardless of the tide's height when you arrive, you can still step down into the tunnel and marvel at its

Tunnel Beach
Tunnel opening
Tunnel Beach Track

peculiar construction. Also, the cliffs, land-bridge and wave spray all combine for a remarkable show, especially during stormy seas.

Down the tunnel

Here's an idea: if you're fretting away another drizzly Dunedin summer day, tired of the "World's steepest road" and the Otago Museum's Plesiosaur (entry E10), maybe head to Tunnel Beach at low tide and bring the coffee/tea kit and a blanket…walk down to the cove, set up inside the dry cave and make some hot drinks as you watch the waves bash at the offshore sea stacks.

DRIVING: Finding Tunnel Beach is tricky. Get a local i-Site map. It's located SE of Dunedin on the bluffs south of St Clair. There's no direct route from downtown, but either from St Clair or SH 1 navigate south and east until you pick up the little brown triangle road pointers indicating the "Southern Scenic Route" to Brighton (Black Head Rd). If your map has Corstorphine Park on it, then you're close…just go 1.7km south of this vast park and you'll find Tunnel Beach Rd.

SE Lakes & Coast

GORGEOUS BEACH COVE, LOTSA WIND, 6PM PENGUINS

Walk: moderate 30-minute (2km) walk down dunes to the Hide

- elevation carpark: 100m
- watch YouTube: egiyvabuy5i & 0sz-dzk_jfk

OBSCUR-O-METER

Sandymount
Penguin Hide
Sandfly Bay Lookout

Sandfly Bay is a force of nature! Arrive during a south wind and you'll immediately understand the name "Sandfly" — the lava cliffs book-ending the beach squeeze the winds into a sand-flying gale. Whoa, there may be more sand in the air than on the beach! No actual sandfly would dare to live here. On a calm day the contoured and swirly-striped dunes are a visual wonderland, but a "sand-flying" windy day is the most impressive as the swirling sand races up the dune channels. If it's ultra-windy and the sand is blasting your face off, simply walk nearer to the waterline to escape the beast.

At the far north end of the beach there's a Yellow-eyed penguin "Hide" for viewing the daily late-afternoon penguin march up the beach. There are enough penguins at this popular beach to warrant a volunteer who'll instruct newbie penguin-watchers on proper pengy-protocol.

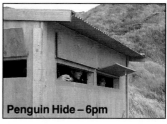

Penguin Hide – 6pm

SE Lakes & Coast

Occasionally there are Sea lions around to liven up the penguin-waiting. One time in 2010 a Sea lion had clambered up to the Hide and was sleeping in front of the door—he seemed kind of friendly in a scary sort of way as he "guarded" the hide. For penguin viewing 6pm (ish) is your best bet…and bring your own binoculars. Penguins nest all along the beach, so you may see one come ashore as you walk to the Hide (sit down and hold still). Amazingly, some penguins make an arduous hop-walk to the top of the hill north of the Hide—look for their faint path up the slope!

DRIVING: Sandfly Bay is signed on the Otago Peninsula Highcliff Rd about 12km from Dunedin, just past Larnach Castle. Turn onto Seal Point Rd to its road-end carpark.

Walk: moderate 40-minute (3 km) loop
- elevation carpark: 240m
- elevation trig: 319m
- watch YouTube: dq0-ex4auoa

OBSCURE · POPULAR
OBSCUR-O-METER

Sandymount's loop track highlights the Otago Peninsula's best views. From the carpark the track ascends 100m to the Sandymount Trig then loops around (counter-clockwise) to visit the cliff-side viewpoints of Lovers Leap and the Chasm before returning.

◀ **Taiaroa Head**

Hooper's inlet from Sandymount

Lover's Leap

This is a nice track, but a bit overgrown with Gorse, so wearing long pants may be a good idea. The views of Otago Peninsula's hills, bays and beaches makes this the peninsula's must-do walking track. At the Trig you'll find a monument with a landscape-identifier plaque which points out what's what on the 360° skyline. From the Trig the track then contours over to the seaside cliffs where both Lovers Leap and the Chasm view-platforms offer precipitous cliff-hanging views. Lovers Leap looks down onto a sort-of sea-arch, whereas the Chasm viewpoint perches above a yawning abyss.

Walk ▶ The loop is marked by DOC arrows. Begin by walking uphill 10 minutes up to Trig. Descend from the Trig and begin the loop—10 minutes to Lovers, 10 more to Chasm, and then 10 more back to the carpark.

Chasm viewpoint

DRIVING: Sandymount Rd is 1km north of Sandfly Bay's Seal Point Rd, then 4 km up this steep unsealed road to its end.

SE Lakes & Coast

ALBATROSS AND PENGUIN VIEWING

Walk: easy, short walks
GORGEOUS DRIVE
• watch Meet the Locals: "Toroa"
• bring: $$ and Albatross-visit reservations

OBSCUR-O-METER

Royal Albatross Ctr

Busy!

The best thing about visiting Taiaroa Head and its popular Royal Albatross Ctr is the scenic drive out the Otago Peninsula. It's best to do the drive as a loop, taking the shoreline road one way and the "Highcliff Rd" route the other. It takes roughly 45-minutes to drive to Taiaroa from Dunedin, and there's no gas available on the peninsula.

The end-of-the-road Royal Albatross Centre is a tourist magnet—expect a huge crowd and "sold-out" ranger-led albatross walks to the world-famous breeding area (about $50pp). From the carpark and nearby areas you may be able to see some soaring albatrosses (but honestly they don't look much different than seagulls when they're just specks in the sky). The free Albatross Center is worth the visit though—it features interesting displays and videos of all sorts of NZ wildlife. The penguin and seal videos

BLUE PENGUIN VIEWING

Penguins can be seen here most evenings (except winter). Many use the steps up from the beach near this area. The penguins come ashore to return to their nests. They usually arrive at dusk (when last light is fading).

Recently penguins have been arriving at about 9:10 pm.

You can help the penguins in this colony by following these simple guidelines...
• No camera flashes
• No torches near penguins
• Be quiet and patient
• Stay behind the fence/wire
• Remember these penguins are wild birds
Dress warmly, and enjoy this special experience.

are fabulous (and a great way to occupy a drizzly day). North of the carpark there's a free view down to a busy Shag breeding colony.

Pilots Bay, underneath the Albatross Ctr, hosts a Blue penguin breeding colony (like Oamaru's, but FREE here). The penguins waddle ashore every night after darkness descends. Often there will be a gaggle of tourists attempting to see these lil blue buggers as they scurry up the short beach

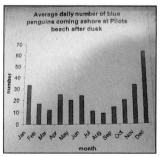

Average daily number of blue penguins coming ashore at Pilots beach after dusk

number

month

before disappearing into the shrubbery. As neat as this sounds, it's a bit frustrating because the penguins often wait until just after dark to come ashore. Too dark for photos and flash pix are a no-no. In January they wait until about 10-10:30pm to come ashore. If you do stay late to watch, stay an extra 30 minutes to hear the penguins begin "sounding-off" in their burrows—it's an eerie cacophony of bizarre screeches.

SE Lakes & Coast

143

The Catlins

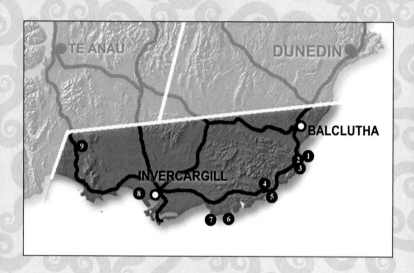

F1 Nugget Pt Lighthouse
F2 Cannibal Bay
F3 Jack's Blowhole
F4 Catlins Waterfalls
F5 Cathedral Caves
F6 Curio Bay
F7 Waipapa Pt Lighthouse
F8 Oreti Beach – Invercargill
F9 Clifden Cave

THE CATLINS

The Catlins were once the South Island's best-kept off-the-beaten-track "secret". The roads were formerly awful and the notorious winds kept all but the hardiest travelers at bay. But no more. A decade or more of the mainstream guidebooks touting the Catlins as "off-the-beaten-track", combined with a strong tourism push by the locals, now means that the Catlins are busy with travelers looking to get away from the other travelers. Don't expect too much solitude in this formerly quiet quarter, but compared to the bustle of Queenstown/Milford, the Catlins will still seem like a wonderful reprieve from rampant Tourism NZ overdose.

The Catlins are definitely worth a visit, and Curio Bay is the show-stopper and best place to stay (my opinion). The mountains are nowhere near as dramatic as Q-town/Wanaka/Fiordland, but when the Roaring 40s winds aren't knocking you down and pushing the trees sideways, the Catlins beaches are some of the finest anywhere on the South Island. Plus, marine wildlife is everywhere! Yellow-eyed penguins are easy to spot, as are the now-plentiful Sea lions. It's fabulous to walk on the Catlins' beaches keeping a sharp eye out for tracks of both penguins and Sea lions in the sand. Savvy travelers who actually read NZ Frenzy will also find the island's best unpublicized chance to spot some Hectors Dolphins…and maybe even swim with some!!

The Catlins also hosts the Island's two most easily-accessed scenic lighthouses at Nugget and Waipapa Pts. Curious travelers can journey out to Slope Pt, the South's true southern-most point, but there's not actually too much to see. Invercargill, the nearest city, doesn't have too much in the way of traveler interest, but if you liked the movie *The World's Fastest Indian*, then make time to nose around Burt Munro's home town for a couple of hours.

F

Watch: YouTube 1k8mjekc0j0

Don't miss:
    Curio Bay!!!!! (7)
    McLeans and Purakaunui Falls (4)

Walk: two easy short walks

- watch YouTube: x1auzg8mep8
- bring: go near 5 pm with binoculars

OBSCUR-O-METER

Nugget's Lighthouse

Nugget Point is the Catlin's famed lighthouse tourist magnet, probably the South Island's most scenic lighthouse location. It's the one with the rocky "nuggets" studding the sea just east of the lighthouse, seen on many a postcard/calendar/brochure. The location seems a photographer's wet dream, as it's super easy to capture the "lonely lighthouse on the wind-swept bluff" feeling, except for the gaggle of tourists that'll often frustrate your foreground. Expect a crowd. Nugget Pt is scenically reminiscent of the North's Cape Reinga, but that's where the similarities end. At Cape Reinga there are tracks and beaches to access and the fascinating spectacle of the two seas overlapping. Nugget Pt has no such offerings. It is basically a tourist photo-op spot with little else to offer—perfect for less-fit or less-adventurous folks, but dull for keen explorers. You do get to see seals swimming below, birds coasting overhead, and lots of kelp doing hula-like swirling around the rocky nuggets. Also, the drive itself to Nugget Pt is fairly scenic along the gravel coastal road from Kaka Point.

The absolute BEST time to visit to visit Nugget Pt is near 5-6pm, when the local Yellow-eyed penguins return to their nests in the little bay below Nugget Pt. This bay—Roaring Bay—gets its name from the ever-present wind, so come prepared. Roaring Bay supports a healthy population of YEPs that hop ashore and then waddle up to their nests every afternoon. There's a Hide building on the hill above the bay which provides a nice sheltered view of where the penguins come ashore—bring binoculars.

Penguin "Hide"

Catlins

DRIVING: From Kaka Point "town" (on the coast south of Balclutha), Nugget Pt is 7km of gravel road to the road-end lighthouse carpark. Just before the road-end is a little roadside carpark for the signed track down to Roaring Bay.

F2 ▶ CANNIBAL BAY

BEACH WALK/DRIVE WITH SEA LIONS

Walk: easy 1-4 km one-way

- watch YouTube: b5qs_ghodjy & s81vjac56bg
- bring: tide chart

OBSCUR-O-METER

Cannibal Bay is a 1km stretch of sand, unremarkable by Catlins standards, except…you can drive on it! Most tourists would never dare, but the beach-drive access is 2WD easy-peasy onto the firmly-packed sands. At the far end of the beach there's a track thru the

Beach access
Driving on Cannibal Beach

grasses that heads over to Surat Bay. Why not have a fun drive to the end of Cannibal's beach and then walk the track over to Surat Bay where you can take a longer walk on the deserted 3km stretch of sand, where you'll

Penguin tracks

almost always spot some lounging Sea lions? Of course you'd need to time this adventure with the tide in mind.

On the drive across the beach look for the obvious tracks from Sea Lions who amble up Cannibal Beach to recline in the grasses. At the far end of the beach you may even find the tracks of some Yellow-eyed penguins that have waddled up the beach to their nests.

Even if the tide is high or you won't risk a beach-drive, the walk is still nice. On the near-side tidal rocks you'll find tide pools a-swirl with copious kelp.

Walk ▶ The marked track to Surat Bay begins at the end of Cannibal and takes 10 minutes to weave over to Surat.

Friendly sea lion
Sea lion tracks

Catlins

DRIVING: The road to Cannibal is a gravel loop road with two access points north of Owaka. From Nugget Point take the "Scenic Route" (south of Kaka) 5km towards Owaka, then turn left onto Ahuriri Flats Rd for 7km gravel to the beach.

From Owaka head north 3km and turn at the Cannibal Bay sign for 8km of gravel to beach.

NICE WALK, LOUSY BLOWHOLE

Walk: easy 18-minute one-way (1.5 km)

- watch YouTube: q0wan79n79w

OBSCURE — POPULAR
OBSCUR-O-METER

Hill of sheep   To blowhole

Jack's Bay

Jack's hole doesn't blow, it sucks. This is probably NZ's only "named" blowhole that doesn't spout at all—it's more of a sea-surge pit than a puffing blowhole. Tourism rah-rah states that the blowhole is located an "astonishing" 200m inland from the sea, but it just doesn't seem very astonishing at all compared to natural wonders like Punakaiki Rocks (C9), or even Sandymount's pits (E14). The bush-clad pit is disappointingly difficult to see down into.

At this point you're thinking, "Fine, we'll skip it"…but wait! The 18-minute track leading to the Jack's hole is a joy, a rare Catlins walking treat! The track ascends a hyper-green hill 'o' sheep then pops up to the

Jack's Sea Lion

headlands ridge where you'll be treated to smashing coastal views. Looking north is Jack's Bay, then Surat Bay, then a wee bit of Cannibal Bay…and finally some Nuggets. Sweet as!

Other than the disappointing blowhole, Jack's Bay, on a sunny day, is a charmer—a low-tide stretch of yellow sand framed by sheer cliffs with explorable tidal shelves at either end. Around to the north you may find an actual blowhole huffing and puffing. Overall, on a sunny day Jack's Bay is worth a visit, just don't expect a riveting natural wonder.

DRIVING: Jack's Bay Rd is signed at the north end of Owaka town – follow the signs 10km of gravel to the beach and road-end carpark.

PHOTOGENIC WATERFALLS

Smallish Catlins waterfalls—nice if you've come down the East Coast, but less impressive if you've just come from Fiordland.

OBSCUR-O-METER

Purakaunui Falls. (Purra-cow-nui) This is the most photogenic of the Catlins waterfalls, one avid waterfall photographers will love. For non-photographers though, the long drive for such a short excursion might not seem worth it. The quick 5-minute track to the falls features some dense jungly bush, but nothing as impressive as McLeans' track.

Purakaunui after heavy rain

Purakaunui drops about 20m in three stairsteps, spreading out horizontally like a pyramid. Anyone who knows how to slow down their shutter speed will turn Purakaunui Falls into a wispy delight. Bring water shoes if you want to hop off the view platform to try for some different photo angles.

Drive: A 14km road loops to the falls from either side of a saddle to the west of Okawa. The first signed turn is 7km west of Okawa at the bay-inlet bridge, and the more western end of the loop is 14.4km west of Okawa. Coming from the west, the first signed loop turn is 25km from Cathedral Caves.

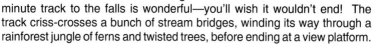

Fun on McLeans Track

McLeans Falls. McLeans Falls is the most dramatic of the Catlins waterfalls, especially after some rain. The falls spill about 20m over a ledge and then cascade down some ledges. The 10-minute track to the falls is wonderful—you'll wish it wouldn't end! The track criss-crosses a bunch of stream bridges, winding its way through a rainforest jungle of ferns and twisted trees, before ending at a view platform.

McCleans Falls

Drive: Falls are signed at the McLeans Falls Holiday Park, 700m west of Cathedral Caves Rd. The Holiday Park is $18pp. Falls are 3km past the Holiday Park on the gravel road.

Matai Falls. This waterfall is mostly just a wee dribbler, located about 5km west of Purakaunui's western loop road. By NZ standards Matai doesn't warrant a stop unless you are truly waterfall-crazed.

Catlins

HUGE SEA CAVES–LOW TIDE ONLY

Walk: easy/moderate 15-minute (1 km) descent to beach
● watch YouTube: treLypdfgdo
● bring: $5pp, sandals, swimsuit, headlamp

OBSCUR-O-METER

Tourists in NZ frustrate the hell outta me. The Cathedral Caves is a case in point. Charge admission in NZ and "they" will come. Huge deep sea caves stud a cliff band on this low-tide only beach. The local Maoris charge $5 pp to access their road and track down to the cave beach. No access to the beach is allowed except for two hours either side of low tide. This rule actually helps people to not be stupid and get bashed by waves as they try to enter the sea-swamped caves at higher tides.

Here's my frustration with typical tourists: the "Cathedral" cave is just a 5-minute beach walk after the 15-minute track descending through the forest to the beach. It seems that about 95% of the people quit right there and stand around taking dull pix of everyone else standing around the mouth of the first big cave. Just around the corner, but with no blinking neon pointing the way, are more caves, deeper caves, further mysteries …but it's the rare traveler who ventures

through the ankle-to-knee deep water to investigate…even just 200m away! Are tourists afraid a rogue wave may bash them against the cliffs? Are they afraid they'll get their calves wet?? Are they afraid because no ticket-taker is there to tell them that there may be something more to see just a few meters away??

Simply scamper over the barnacled rocks and you'll find more caves and way less people. How many footprints do you see? Probably none. The only person I've seen past the first cave was a frightened little penguin chirping at me in the far back of the dark cave (I was as scared as he!) Then, another 200m over another tidal shelf and through more knee-deep wave-slosh comes a beach cove with…nope, I won't tell…but it did inspire stripping off the togs for a rousing rinse! The walk back to the main cave from this "off-the-beaten-track" cove took all of 8 minutes, and sadly, back

Catlins

Cave openings

One sea lion, many tourists

at the first cave there were 40 people aimlessly milling about. Don't people come to NZ to explore??

Given that you bought my book, I know that you're adventurous. This is the reason I've written this guide. I hope to lend some insight on these sorts of places and encourage you to be a bit prepared to leave the beaten path.

Come and see the caves. Be warned that the carpark may have 30-90 cars! If you're an explorer try to arrive 1-2 hours before low-tide. Wear a swimsuit and water sandals and slosh past the first cave before true low tide (when other people might try the same). You'll find some neat exploring beyond.

Caves past the first ones

Catlins

DRIVING: The caves are signed on Southern Route Rd, 40km west from Okawa or 33km east from Curio Bay, nearly adjacent to McLean Falls Holiday Park.

F6 ▷ CURIO BAY

JURASSIC PLAYGROUND WITH FRIENDLY MINI-DOLPHINS

- watch YouTube: ep8waL4pvdq; x2z3naxuLdc & bpebjgs3cje
- watch Meet the Locals: "Camping with Nature"; "Hectors Dolphins" & "Petrified Forest"

OBSCUR-O-METER

There's nowhere else on our planet like Curio Bay. A strong statement, yes, but there's simply nowhere else in the world that you can watch happy-hour penguins hop atop barnacle-encrusted petrified tree stumps after an afternoon of surfing with friendly mini-dolphins......read on.

Curio Bay's main claim-to-fame is its large tidal shelf replete with a 170-million-year-old petrified-stump forest which pokes up out of it. This ancient forest was petrified as it once stood, and nowadays each stump has a cone of mud around it, making them look like little volcanoes. There are also petrified logs lying cross-wise amongst the stumps. At full high tide the shelf is flooded-over, but anytime else you can easily walk down amongst this bizarre Jurassic park. Ever seen a barnacle-encrusted petrified stump?

Campground

Petrified stumps

The BEST time to explore Curio Bay is between 6-8pm when the resident colony of Yellow-eyed penguins comes ashore for the night. Watching the Curio Bay penguin parade is remarkably better than at the other sites up the coast towards Oamaru. First, there's no "Hide" and you are free to wander around the Jurassic tidal-shelf and perch your butt on a petrified stump to watch the nightly waddle. Secondly, the penguins of Curio seem habituated to human presence, so they don't retreat at the sight of a human. During "hoppy hour" the penguins pop out of the surf (a bit left/east of the view platform) and preen a bit before rock-hopping to their bush-line nests. These are the best penguin photo-ops you'll EVER get! Once in their nests, the

6pm penguin parade

Catlins

penguins often screech and call, just adding more bizarre to this bizarrest of locales.

Curio Bay also harbors a little-known "secret"...shhhh. Porpoise Bay begins just around the Curio Bay headland. Porpoise Bay is a long crescent of sand so-named for its resident Hectors Dolphins. These rare mini dolphins live in-shore and spend their lives in this bay. Thus, the local Hectors' have become quite accustomed to humans and they're super friendly to surfers and swimmers!! The trick though is that the water is Antarctic-cold, so you'll need a wetsuit to spend any length of time in the water.

Fortunately, at the campground, Catlins Surf will kit you out with wetsuit, booties and surfboard for about $50/3 hours. Nick cannot rent you just a wetsuit, as then he'd become a "dolphin encounter" operation (all sorts of permitting and regulations...and tourist publicity). Thus, he's solely a low-key surfboard rental/lessons operation, not attempting to publicize the rare "surf-with-dolphins" opportunity. Most Catlins tourists hurry elsewhere where there's more publicity, but now that you know you'll stay, wait for the wind to stop, hire a board, or maybe take a lesson with some playful Hectors to "hang ten" with!

Imagine the story you'll tell at home of the Jurassic bay where you belly-rode a surfboard amidst a pod of friendly mini-dolphins, then watched an up-close penguin parade while perched on a petrified stump! Nowhere in the Catlins is as cool as Curio...don't hurry away.

Camping: The Curio Bay Camping Ground has one of the sweetest spots on the island. No sandflies! Quick walk to both Curio and Porpoise Bays, with a cliff-top sunset overlook to boot! Extra fun is when friendly young Sea Lions invade the camp to tussle. About $15 pp.

Watch videos!!!

NEVER APPROACH A DOLPHIN
Let them come to you

South Head

30m

Beach signs

Swimmers
If you can see dolphins;
Enter the water at least 30m away,
preferably between the dolphins and South Head.

DRIVING: Curio Bay is signed off the Southern Scenic Route. FYI, the 32km gravel road from Fortrose via Waipapa Lighthouse/ Slope Pt is a good road.

THE BEST "LAND'S END" SPOT TO VISIT

- Lighthouse
- Shipwreck
- Wind Shelter info kiosk
- Cemetery
- Sea Lions

OBSCURE — POPULAR
OBSCUR-O-METER

The Waipapa Point Lighthouse is the southernmost lighthouse on the South Island, and even though it's not quite as south as Slope Point, it's more interesting to visit Waipapa than the no-frills no-interest Slope Pt*. The Waipapa Lighthouse is also a good bit more south than the way-touristy signpost at Bluff's Stirling Point*.

At the Waipapa Lighthouse you may also see some beached Sea Lions and some of those classic windswept Catlins trees. There's also a newly-created wind shelter info-kiosk that displays a bunch of interesting historic panels. The panels and historic photos detail the history of the lighthouse and its keepers as well as the tragic 1881 shipwreck of the "Tararua" in which an incredible 131 out of 151 passengers died just 1km offshore. If you enjoy a bit of history, then read the panels and then also visit the "Tararua Acre" cemetery which is signposted a couple kms back on the gravel road at the turn.

Sea lions on lighthouse beach

You'll need to walk a couple minutes across the paddock to the fenced "Acre" where you'll find an info panel describing an even better account of the torturous wreck and a scattering of some lonely gravestones.

Catlins

154

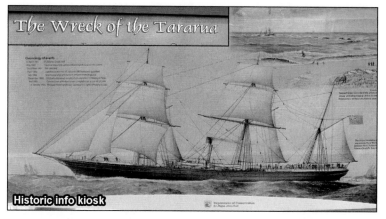

The Wreck of the Tararua

Historic info kiosk

WAIPAPA LIGHTHOUSE RD
NO EXIT

Tararua Acre
400m walk

Waipapa Point

FYI ▶ If you're further interested in shipwrecks, the Catlins coast had many, but the ONLY visible remains are of the SS Ino, still visible at low tide inside the Fortrose estuary. Immediately south of Fortrose there's a road sign pointing the way, and inside the Fortrose info-pub there's a shipwreck booklet that has the details.

In Okawa, at the i-Site museum, there are also shipwreck videos played in the theater.

Shipwreck (not visible)

SHIPWRECK INO VISIBLE AT LOW TIDE

In Fortrose

*FYI ▶ If you're wondering if the long drive to see Bluff's Stirling Pt is worth it...I don't think so. Stirling Pt is not even near the southern tip of Bluff, let alone the southern-most point of NZ. Simply Google-Image "Bluff" and you'll see all the tourist pics of the tourist signpost that you need to see.

As for Slope Pt, it's not too interesting either. If you're "killing time" waiting for Curio's penguin march, then maybe have a look at Slope, but be warned that there's nothing there of interest but a signpost. Just Google Image it, then get to Curio and look for some Hectors surfing the waves!!

Catlins

DRIVING: The Waipapa Lighthouse is located between Fortrose and Curio Bay on the gravel Scenic route. This route is 32km of good gravel roads, signed the entire way. The signed turn for Waipapa is 12km from Fortrose or 21km from Curio Bay. The lighthouse is an extra 5km off the Scenic route.

F8 ORETI BEACH/INVERCARGILL

(oh-ready)

HOME TO BURT MUNRO, "THE WORLD'S FASTEST INDIAN"

Drive: Burt's original racing beach

- watch YouTube: g_uvcu_8zds; kjkd_gfvjky; xxyx69q6qve; npqqsf7-pzs
- bring: tide chart

OBSCURE POPULAR
OBSCUR-O-METER

Invercargill is home to *The World's Fastest Indian*, both the movie and motorcycle. In the much-loved movie Sir Anthony Hopkins stars as local hero Burt Munro who purchased an Indian motorcycle in 1920 and then spent the next 50 years racing and re-engineering it until taking it to America to set international speed records, much to the shocked surprise of the Bonneville Salt Flats "speed" scene. Burt was a quintessential small-town Kiwi who made a big splash on the world stage. Nowadays, though Burt passed-away in 1979, Invercargill's favorite son is still a national hero.

If you love the movie, as most everyone does, then don't just drive through Invercargill...**Go drive on Burt's original racetrack—Oreti Beach!** This beach, located 10km west of town, is probably the easiest drive-upon beach anywhere in New Zealand. The pavement ends directly onto the wet sands of the beach where there are vast expanses of cement-like sands to drive on. Head north, STEP ON IT, and take a 10km cruise up to the Waimatuku Stream and turn around. Don't be an idiot—drive above the waves and below the dry sand. Don't worry about the crunching shells. To find Oreti Beach turn onto Tweed St. at the south end of Invercargill and head 10km west to the beach.

Drive the beach!

If you like the story of Burt Munro and his World's Fastest Indian you MUST pop into ***E. Hayes & Sons LTD*** hardware store on the main street through Invercargill (Dee and Leet). Mr. Hayes was a friend of Burt's and now owns and showcases Burt's actual two record-setting motos as well as a neat collection of other antique bikes. Get a t-shirt, a

The real moto!

E. Hayes & Sons Hardware

postcard, or sticker, and get a good look at the relic of a bike that an ole' Burt made run faster than it ever should have!

Also, in the nearby Southland Museum there's a Burt Munro showcase. A 26-minute movie runs showing the actual life and times of Burt as he ventured to America in the 1960s in pursuit of world speed records (this film is also often included on the DVD version of *The World's Fastest Indian*). The film is a fantastic homage to a small-town Kiwi who dreamed big and then had the verve to make his dreams of speed records and world travel come true.

If you've seen the movie, you may be interested in Tim Hanna's biography *One Good Run: The Legend of Burt Munro.* Whereas the movie basically recounts the 6 months of Burt's life when he first took his motorcycle to America to set his first record, the book tells the entire story of Burt's younger life, his life-long obsession with the Indian, and his many trips and love affair with all things America.

From the book: "Bert Munro was a stubborn old miser who cadged, cajoled, wheedled, charmed and occasionally begged for anything he needed to make his old machine go faster. Why anyone would want to take a 1920 Indian Scout, a fine machine in its day but no rocket, and turn it into an alcohol-burning fire-breather to attack international speed records almost half a century later, at speeds almost four times those it had been capable of when new, was not a question the old rider had ever bothered with much. In fact, the idea of breaking records was fairly extraneous to the exercise. He did what he did mainly because meeting the challenge gave him more satisfaction than anything else, with the possible exception of an encounter with a willing woman."

Catlins

UNDERGROUND ADVENTURE!!

Tramp: difficult one-hour scramble
- watch YouTube: qgLdky2wrs0
- bring: two lights minimum, at least one per person, rugged clothing

OBSCURE — POPULAR
OBSCUR-O-METER

Welcome to
CLIFDEN CAVES

The Clifden Cave is probably the South Island's least-known public cave adventure. It seems that this cave is a casualty of NZ's more-commercialized modern "beaten" tourist path. Clifden, as the plaque at the entrance describes, was a popular stop for tourists dating back to the 1890s. Nowadays though, given its free and uncommercialized nature, the cave has fallen "off the map"…literally. Clifden (or Waiau) Cave is rarely highlighted on typical NZ map guides, and though the cave is featured in a DOC brochure, the brochure is almost impossible to find except at the Te Anau VisCtr. Thanks for getting my book…hope you're having fun!

So, Clifden Cave is a fun underground adventure, similar to Cave Stream's excursion (B8). What makes this cave unique is that it makes an underground loop as you clamber, squeeze, climb, and splash a route through this cave's wonderful labyrinth.

LIMESTONE CAVES

Entrance hole

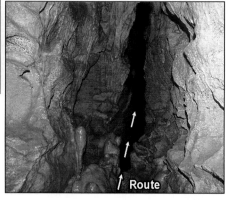

↑
↑
↑ Route

I won't ruin the surprise of this cave for you by telling every detail…I just hope to excite you enough that you'll stop for a 90-120-minute adventure and be prepared. The cave entrance and exit are only 300m apart, directly on the paved road…but you'll have to travel about a mile under-ground to cover the

Catlins

300m between entrance and exit. The cave is difficult, but no more so than the typical Kiwi tramping route. It does require ducking, crouching, and a wee bit of crawl and climb here and there, but mostly you simply walk the labyrinthine passages. The route through the cave is clearly marked by DOC arrows. The cave does drip and there are puddles and mud. You will get dirty hands, knees, elbows, and bum. Expect about an hour underground. It's chilly in the cave, so wear long pants, long sleeves, water shoes/sandals and maybe a

Route

Cave pool

winter hat. **Two lights are minimum (if your lights die in this cave, you'll die with them—bring extra lights!)! (!)**

For cave-loving folks, this cave delivers! Each step gets better and better. You'll see signatures galore from centuries past as well as all the limestone cave goodies—stalactites and stalagmites, flowstone and "bacon", soda straws, angel wings, and even a helictite or two. Sadly, the pioneers laid waste to the original delicacies of Clifden Cave, but there's still enough to awe. I won't say any more to ruin the surprises…but you will be SURPRISED! This is a fun caving adventure full of unexpected twists and turns! For folks who don't like caves, then just skip this one, as there's nothing impressive to see at the entrance except a plaque detailing the cave's historic significance.

Photography in the cave is fairly easy, but carrying a good camera and tripod isn't easy. A backpack will be a curse in the tight passages. A small pocket flash camera is best. Did I tell you about the waterfall and the pool? Oops, I'll shut up…if you're an adventurer, don't miss this one!

Catlins

DRIVING: The Clifden Cave is signed on the Southern Scenic Route (SH 99) just north of the historic Clifden suspension bridge. It's 85km south of Te Anau or 14km north of Tuatapere. North of the bridge 1km there's a stop-sign road junction with cave signage. Go east here just 500m then turn onto the Clifden Gorge Rd for 1km to the small yellow cave sign and roadside parking.

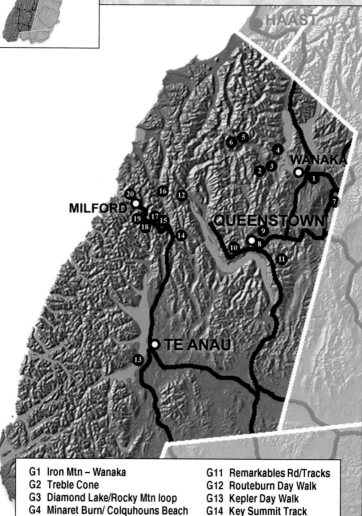

G1 Iron Mtn – Wanaka
G2 Treble Cone
G3 Diamond Lake/Rocky Mtn loop
G4 Minaret Burn/ Colquhouns Beach
G5 Glacier Burn Valley
G6 Rob Roy Glacier Valley
G7 Bendigo Ghost Town
G8 Queenstown Hill Walkway
G9 Shotover River Canyon
G10 Mt Crichton Loop
G11 Remarkables Rd/Tracks
G12 Routeburn Day Walk
G13 Kepler Day Walk
G14 Key Summit Track
G15 Marian Lake Track
G16 Humboldt Falls
G17 Gertrude Valley Track
G18 Homer Tunnel Ice Field
G19 The Chasm
G20 Milford Sound

WANAKA, QUEENSTOWN, MILFORD SOUND

The southwest corner of the South Island, encompassing the Queenstown/Wanaka lakes area as well as Te Anau and Fiordland Nat'l Park, packs the most scenic bang-for-the-buck in New Zealand.

Queenstown and Wanaka are both blessedly sunny, being both situated on the dry side of the Fiordland and Mt Aspiring mountains. Both towns are gorgeous, yet very different—see pages 162 and 174 for details. An extra bonus to both towns is that they don't suffer the plague of sandflies that inflict insanity at both Fiordland and the wet West Coast. If the sandflies are driving you mad, then count on Q-town or Wanaka to be a welcome relief!

As for Fiordland Nat'l Park and Milford/Doubtful Sounds…they need little hoopla given that they are a World Heritage Site and oft-ranked as one of the world's top wonder-spots. Milford Sound and the Fiordlands drive definitely rank up there with the USA's Grand Canyon and Yosemite…possibly outdoing both!

Rainy Milford

The Milford Track is often referred to as being referred-to one of the finest walks in the world, but the planning and expense it entails, combined with the worst weather and worst sandflies, makes most in-the-know trampers much prefer the mountainous Routeburn. But the drive to Milford Sound, as the road enters the mountains for the final 40km, is one jaw-drop sight after another without any major plannings nor expense. Local Tourism bureaus may try to make travelers believe that clouds and rain on the road to Milford enhance its "mystical" charm…but that's hogwash. Without a doubt you want to see Fiordland in the sunshine if you can, so it's good to plan at least a few days in the area so you can race towards Milford whenever the forecast looks best. On average, it rains in Milford about half the days of the year, with an average of about .75 inches of rain per summer day (28 inches in January!) Bring a raincoat, bring the DEET…but if your time on the South Island is limited, then plan to spend the majority down here!

"Mystic" Milford

Watch: Meet the Locals: "Shadowlands", and "Milford Track"

Don't Miss:
   Queenstown's Glenorchy & Remarkables Drives (11, 12)
   Rob Roy Glacier (6)
   Milford Sound Drive (20)
   Key Summit Track (14)

Best Milford

G

WANAKA (Wanna-ka)

Watch: YouTube: oeweg00d_xa

- elevation: 345m

This page about Wanaka, in conjunction with page 174 about Queenstown, are an attempt to give travelers a bit of info and perspective about these two well-known, but very different, destination towns.

Wanaka is sort of a beach town, but one set amidst gorgeous mountains. Wanaka is low-key, quiet and natural compared to Queenstown's busy-busy hustle-bustle. For most travelers time in Wanaka revolves around its lakefront beaches....think swimming, tanning, reading, and sunning...all just a few steps from Wanaka's small-town shops, cafes, and hotels. Unlike most lakes on the South Island, Lake Wanaka warms-up enough in the summer for delightful swimming. Combine the warm water, easy-access beach, lack of sandflies, and sunny days...and you've got the first reason to break out the bikini since the Abel Tasman. Sweet as!

Wanaka doesn't have high-rise condos, parking garages, nor nightclubs and "nightlife". People flock to Queenstown for partying and excitement, whereas people in Wanaka relax and enjoy the simple natural beauty. There are plenty of walks/drives/explorations to be had in and around Wanaka, but very few commercialized adventures/tours/rides/etc compared to Queenstown.

There are two main publicized "attractions" in Wanaka. The first is *Puzzling World*, which offers a world-class fun-for-all-ages adventure maze, as well as a gift-shop and mini-museum of mind-bending oddities. *Puzzling World* is the must-see bad-weather-day option.

The second place is *Cinema Paradiso*, which is a small idiosyncratic movie house. This theater features food and drink, both first-run and quirky off-beat movies, and a very fun and entertaining ambience. It seems that every Kiwi on the South Island has caught a flick at the renowned *Cinema Paradiso*!

Wanaka,Q-town,Milford

G1 ▶ IRON MOUNTAIN

WANAKA'S TOWN HILL

Walk: moderate 60-minute (5 km) loop

- elevation trailhead: 300m
- elevation top: 545m

OBSCUR-O-METER

Iron Mtn is Wanaka's "town mountain", though it's more of a hill than any sort of mountain. A well-maintained 5km track ascends to the peak and then loops back down to the start. Everyone in Wanaka, from old to young, has walked the loop, and you should too. If your travels only allow you one hour for a walk in Wanaka, then Iron Mtn is your best option.

Treble Cone

Matukituki Valley

Plaque

Iron Mountain Trig

A Trig marks the top of the "mountain" and sports a killer 360° view. It also has a mountain-identifier plaque that'll point out all the Wanaka-area skyline features. From the viewpoint Lake Wanaka stretches northwards while the Stevenson Arm's Dublin Bay gives birth to the Clutha River. To the north you'll see a wee slice of Lake Hawea, while over your other shoulder is a look towards Cardrona's ski field road. Encircling Iron Mtn below is every bit of both Wanaka and Albert Town—so bring the binoculars if you want to spot your house/hotel/camp spot. Make sure to check out Puzzling World's maze from above—maybe you can discover some secrets with this bird's eye view.

Puzzling World

DRIVING: Two carparks are located a couple of kms south of Wanaka. It's best to park at the one across from Puzzling World because there's shade. From there walk the loop clockwise, heading left to start.

Wanaka,Q-town,Milford

G2 TREBLE CONE

SCENIC SKI-FIELD ROAD AND DOUBLE WATERFALL

Walk: easy 1 km walk to base of waterfall

• watch Meet the Locals: "Treble Cone Vandals"
• bring: sandals

OBSCURE — POPULAR
OBSCUR-O-METER

Treble Cone is Wanaka's mountain-top ski resort. Like Queenstown's Remarkables drive (G11), you can drive up Treble Cone's steep gravel access road simply as a

View from Treble Cone

Wanaka

Iron Mtn

sight-seer. In summertime you'll probably see some paragliders floating down from Treble Cone's heights. Unlike the Remarkables Rd that sports jaw-drop views from the get-go, you need to drive fairly far up Treble Cone

TREBLE CONE

Twin waterfalls

before you can see over Rocky Mtn to Lake Wanaka. Truth-be-told, the top of Rocky Mtn has a much better view than Treble Cone, but for people not up for the rugged Rocky Mtn hike, then the Treble Cone drive is your ticket.

Directly in front of Treble Cone's lower entrance gate is **a pair of thousand-foot waterfalls spilling down the cliff face—quite a sight.** The one on the left has a nice grotto at its base where the stream makes its final 25m leap into a shallow pool…yay! If you're up for a shower at the base of a gargantuan waterfall, then park at Treble's entrance gate, go left thru the tall fence gate, and then follow the stream bank for 12 minutes up to the sunny and private nook at the base of the lefthand waterfall.

Waterfall shower

DRIVING: Treble Cone's access road (and waterfalls) is 22km west of Wanaka, past Glendhu Bay towards Matukituki Valley/Rob Roy Glacier.

G3 ▶ DIAMOND LAKE/ROCKY MOUNTAIN LOOP TRACK

EXCELLENT VIEWPOINT

Walk: difficult 2-hour semi-loop (8km), with shorter options

- watch Meet the Locals: "Diamond Lake"
- elevation trailhead: 330m; elev top: 775m

OBSCUR-O-METER

Rocky Mtn. View

Colq-Beach Track

Matukituki River

Rocky Mountain is a bit like Iron Mtn except it's both higher and more demanding...and the view is substantially better! There's a loop track to the top of Rocky Mtn which passes historic Diamond Lake on the way up. The track is a demanding hour-long climb featuring both steep steps and rocky sections. But wow, the top viewpoint is impressive indeed! You'll have earned a rest when you reach the top, and to be sure, there's plenty of 360° glory to feast your eyes on.

Glendhu Bay and the shingled mouth of the Matukituki River are immediately below. To the north glaciated peaks dominate the skyline with pointy 3,033m Mt Aspiring crowning them all. To the west you'll get a full view of Treble Cone from top to bottom. Looking SW the Motatapu Stream winds its way west through singer Shania Twain's vast green "Soho station". And yes, of course, Lake Wanaka sprawls below from Island Mou Waho to Wanaka town and the wee bump of Iron Mtn behind it. Impressive indeed!

Apparently, gratitude for the track goes to Puzzling World's Stuart Landsborough who spent years constructing and maintaining this track. The mapboard at the carpark details the area's history as well as showing the routes and options.

Wanaka

Roy's Peak

Glendhu Bay

The best way to the top is counter-clockwise via the eastern route—it sports better views while you stop to catch your breath.

Walk ▶ There are many options here, as the mapboard in the carpark details. The lake is easy, but not especially notable. The Lake Wanaka Viewpoint is a nice vantage for folks who don't want to sweat their way to the top.

DRIVING: The signed "Diamond Lake Conservation Area" is 19km NW of Wanaka, 6km past Glendhu Bay.

G4 MINARET BURN/COLQUHOUNS BEACH TRACK

OFF-THE-BEATEN-TRACK SHORELINE

Walk: easy 90-minute (7km) one-way

● bring: lighter, paper, BBQ food

OBSCURE · POPULAR

OBSCUR-O-METER

Welcome to Minaret Burn Track

Nau mai, haere mai, tauti mai

This little-known track tours one of the rare publicly accessible, yet undeveloped, shorelines of Lake Wanaka. Fabulous lake/mountain views greet each turn of the track the entire route. On a warm calm sunny Wanaka day this remote track to Colquhouns Beach is a dream come true, as the surroundings are 100% pure NZ—not a house in sight! Unlike most of the tracks near Wanaka, this one doesn't require any steep climbing—it simply ungulates about 7km along the sparse hillsides about 100m above the lake before finally escorting you onto the mile-long Colquhouns Beach. The walk is mostly on an old farm road, which is good—the wide flat surface allows your gaze to wander over the mountains and coves and blue-blue lake without having to watch your steps. Arriving at Colquhouns Beach you'll find a long scenic sweep of white-pebbled "beach" with mountains all around and Mou Waho Island front and center in Lake Wanaka. Mou Waho is the famed island which has a lake upon the island which has islands in the little lake. From the beach 2,339m Mt Alta peeks from high left. There's more driftwood on the beach than you could burn in a lifetime, so maybe bring hotdogs and a lighter for a fun BBQ picnic. The odd boat may venture past, but chances are that it'll be just you on this heavenly reach.

Carpark

Track

1st swim cove

Wanaka,Q-town,Milford

If you're not up for a 7km one-way walk and maybe want an easier outing, then Homestead Bay, where the track begins, is a nice spot to picnic where the Matukituki River pours into the lake. Also, along the track just 10 minutes is an accessible swimming cove—the only one on the Colquhouns route.

Track views over lake

This track would make a great overnight backpack excursion—at Colquhouns you'll find flats for tents and plenty of wood to burn. Also, this track is a gem for Mtn bikes or trail runners.

Walk ▶ There's a mapboard at the carpark showing the route, but the map states that Colquhouns is only 4km away. It's wrong—the beach is more like 4 miles, or 7km, taking a solid 90-minute one-way walk. The short path to the down to the actual beach is signed towards the northern end of the bay.

Colquhoun's Beach

DRIVING: Head west of Wanaka 17km towards and past Glendhu Bay. You're looking for West Wanaka Rd, which is 4.5km past Glendhu Bay. Turn right onto gravel West Wanaka Rd and follow it 5km through some gates to the road-end carpark.

G5 GLACIER BURN VALLEY

ROB ROY'S SECRET COUSIN

**Walk/tramp: mod/diff 75 minutes (6km)
one-way—45-minute flat, 30-minute steeps**

• elevation trailhead: 300m
• elevation high point on ridge: 600m

OBSCURE — POPULAR

OBSCUR-O-METER

The Glacier Burn track heads into the heart of a huge glacier-topped valley, ending alongside the Glacier Burn stream with distant views of a massive glacial wall and its lovely waterfalls. These are the glaciers and waterfalls that you see on the drive up the Matukituki River towards Rob Roy. Don't opt for this track instead of the Rob Roy track—without doubt Rob Roy is more impressive. But, if you've seen Rob Roy and want to spend some more private/solitary time in a glacial valley, then this is a good option. Rob Roy's carpark will have 50 cars whereas Cameron Flat may have one. Glacier Burn is the place to find a flat stream-side schist boulder, doff the clothing, and bask in 100% pure, 100% off-the-beaten-track, nobody-around-for-miles New Zealand splendor.

For extra fun pack along some beers and stash them in the icy Glacier Burn stream at the end of the long walk through the paddocks (before the steep climb up and over the ridge). Thus, on the walk out, to accompany the long dull-ish walk back to the car, you'll have something to toast the wonders of Wanaka with. ☺

Walk/Tramp The track begins by crossing the Matukituki River at Cameron Flat. Wear sandals to start and walk by crossing the stream wherever it seems knee-deep. Keep the sandals on until you get to the

Glacier Burn Valley

Matukituki River

Cameron Flat

Hanging Glacier

Glacier Burn Valley

trees, because there may be more shallow crossings. (You won't need the sandals again, so stash them near the farm gate for the return trip and lace up the boots.)

The marked route now heads along the farm road and then along the farm fences for about 40 dull minutes until you get to the Glacier Burn Stream. At the stream there's a DOC sign pointing left for the Burn track, but first take a peek at the swingbridge spanning the gorge (and find a spot for your beers). Head left from the sign following the arrows for a steep 20-minute (250m vertical) tramp up the slope to the saddle where you'll then descend 10 minutes down to the track-end. As you begin the descent, one minute over the saddle, next to a big stump, look carefully through the trees for a great view of the valley's waterfalls. Where the track ends at the Glacier Burn Stream the views are a little disappointing, but a quick rock-hop upstream will reveal better sights (oddly, the further you go up the stream, the worse the views get—just go 5 minutes.)

On the way back out, after collecting your libations, instead of immediately backtracking through the paddocks, maybe follow the glacial stream to its joining with the East Matukituki River. From there follow along the bank of the East Matukituki for better variety and better views before cutting thru the paddock back to the farm road.

DRIVING: From Wanaka head towards Treble Cone and Rob Roy. When the road becomes gravel set your odometer. The signed turn for Cameron Flat is 24km into the gravel drive to Rob Roy carpark (8km before Rob Roy.) Turn right and go a short way until the road ends at the river.

G6 ▶ ROB ROY GLACIER VALLEY TRACK

HANGING GLACIER SHANGRI-LA VALLEY

Walk/tramp: mod/diff 80-min (6km) one-way
- elev carpark: 375m; viewpoint: 800m
- watch YouTube: 7zLpLnn-ige
- bring: water shoes for extra exploring

OBSCUR-O-METER

The Rob Roy Glacier-view trailhead is a long gravel drive from Wanaka…is it worth it? Yes, emphatically yes. Other than Mt Cook's Hooker Valley Track, the Rob Roy Glacier viewpoint may be the WOW-est day-walk viewpoint in the Southern Alps. **Put this track on the must-see list!!**

Matukituki River swing bridge

The track first runs alongside the ice-blue Matukituki River before swinging you across for the climb into the Beech-clad Rob Roy Valley. As you now climb up through the thickly-forested valley you'll be accompanied with the constant roar of whitewater below. After a pre-emptive view of a knock-your-socks-off impressive ribbon of waterfall, you'll arrive at the final viewpoint…and WHOA! A panoramic glacial amphitheatre of indescribable

1000 feet!

majesty unfolds before your eyes!! Waterfalls roar all around, pouring off the blue tongues of Rob Roy's snowy heights. Jagged peaks encircle the valley while wildflowers carpet the floor under foot. To top off the umph, as you sit pondering the juggernaut enormity of the scene, a friendly Kea may fly up, check out your zippers and have a munch on the nearby wildflower buds. If you're lucky enough to have your eyes peeled when the glacier calves a huge thunderous hunk…well, good on ya! Bring lunch and expect to spend at least an hour at the trail's end viewpoint!

The Rob Roy Glacial amphitheater is impressive[2]! I can't praise it enough. At most view-points you get an eye-full and then that's enough (Milford, Franz Josef, etc). But at Rob Roy the scene captivates with its constantly changing nature…the 1000-foot waterfall wisps back and forth, the Keas fly, swoop, call and land, the waterfalls roar, the glacier calves. This is riveting NZ wilderness! **In a nutshell, don't miss this spot!!**

Flower-eating Kea

Walk ▶ From the carpark it's 15 minutes of easy walking to the scenic swingbridge. From there the trail steepens considerably for 25 minutes of roots and rocks, then moderates for the final 40 minutes to the trail's end view-rocks. After a large eye-full of glacier-rama and Kea lovin', maybe head down a few minutes to the rushing stream for a different vantage.

FYI ▶ You can get over to and under the huge wispy waterfall, but it's not easy. Wade the stream, push through the brush/bush, up the marshy grass…and you'll be rainbowed under one of the South Island's highest pure free falls.

Rob Roy Glacier

DRIVING: Map and restrooms at trailhead. It's a 54km drive from Wanaka to the road-end trailhead, the last 32km washboardy gravel. It takes an hour to drive from Wanaka, *if you drive fast (60-80km/hr)* on the washboard road. If you can't/won't drive a gravel washboard road at high speed, then the journey to Rob Roy will be a tortuously slow chore. Drive fast, smooth out the bumps and be at the road-end carpark in an hour. Drive slow, then two hours. Larger Motorhomes/RVs may want to think twice about the arduous drive.

Wanaka,Q-town,Milford

HISTORIC GOLD-MINING RUINS

Walk: various short explorations

● bring: Walk Cromwell Brochure

OBSCURE / POPULAR
OBSCUR-O-METER

Bendigo hosts the remains of what was, in the 1870s, the single biggest mining success story in NZ history. Half a million pounds of gold were extracted from the area's hard-rock quartz reefs—the greatest fortune EVER made in NZ. It'd be hard to tell from the lonely wind-swept remains that the Bendigo boom town, with its nearby Logantown/Welshtown neighbors, was once the talk of New Zealand.

Mandatory for a good visit is the Cromwell local _Walk Cromwell brochure_ available at area i-Sites (Queenstown, Arrowtown, Wanaka, Cromwell). This map has detailed walking routes and scads of historic info. Make sure you find one because without it the trip will be rather lifeless. There is a DOC brochure, but it's pretty dull—make sure to get Cromwell's free brochure.

A scattering of visible ruins, remains and remnants are easily seen on a one-hour walking tour of the ghost town area. You'll see the crumbling walls of roofless cabins and even the 5-star Pengelly Hotel. A loop track tours other mining ruins including a stamper battery site and some intriguing deep-deep-deep fenced-over mine shafts. When the loop swings by Shaft #2, its deep dark deep dark deepness will awe you—it's an astounding 178 meters deep! (For perspective, AJ Hackett's Kawarau Bungy is 42m and takes about 3 seconds to make the plunge. Here at Shaft #2, the drop is

5+ seconds! **Try the math....If a 1lb rock is dropped and takes 5.5 seconds to thud at the bottom, then the equation, Distance = Velocity x Time^2 says the distance fallen is ???? (The velocity of a dropped object is roughly 5m/sec^2, thus Dist = 5 x Time^2. You try!)**

The Bendigo/Logantown/Welshtown ruins are far off the beaten path. Chances are that you'll see few people, but plenty of ghosts. If you want to see some "real" NZ history instead of some commercialized historical re-enactment like Greymouth's Shantytown, then make time for about a 90-minute detour on the journey between Wanaka and Queenstown.

Walk ▶ First thing, find the Pengelly Hotel so you can see what 5-star meant in 1870! It's up the road from the carpark another 100m and off to the left across the gully. Then, begin walking past the signed Welshtown

ruins to pick up the marked loop route. Simply waltz past the Matilda sign and you're on your way (sorry, I just had to write that. How often do you get to waltz past a Matilda?)

DRIVING: There are two gravel roads into Bendigo from SH 8 north of Cromwell. From Cromwell head 15km north, turn at The Stables and go 3.5km. Coming from the north the Bendigo Loop Rd is signed 8km south of Wanaka's Hwy 8a junction—turn left at the sign and go 4km. These two gravel roads meet at the current "Bendigo", which is just a home and some ruins. From this corner junction an interpretive sign will point you upwards another 3.5km to the Welshtown road-end carpark (head up the steep rough hill past the vineyard sign.)

QUEENSTOWN...the town

Watch: YouTube: gwtpijLcfrc

● elevation: 357M

Queenstown is the internationally-known ski-town and adventure-mecca of New Zealand. Q-town throbs with a young, energetic, excited vibe. Whereas most NZ small towns lean towards the sleepy side, Queenstown breaks the mold in a BIG way! Both Kiwis and travelers flock to Queenstown for the "action"...the skiing/bungy/jet boat/ whitewater rafting, the open-til-late nightclubs, the acclaimed restaurants. Like Wanaka, Queenstown is located on a gorgeous lakeside setting, but that's where the similarity ends. Queenstown's lakefront airport whooshes visitors in from far and wide and houses the holidaying hordes in a myriad of hi-

rise condos and hotels. This city is all about playing, shopping, dining, and drinking in the Fast Lane! You don't come to Queenstown to chill-out, you come to live fast, play hard, and be excited!

This is not to say Queenstown doesn't have its free natural beauty and charm...because it does, in spades! The town is set along gorgeous Lake Wakatipu with the craggy Remarkables Mountains as the stunning backdrop. Any drive you take is eye-candy in every direction!! Do not make the mistake of thinking Queenstown is solely the home to manufactured entertainment like bungying and jet boats, because Queenstown's oft-unheralded natural beauty is second to none in NZ. You can visit Queenstown and have an excellent time even if you don't want to spend a dime on the uber-publicized thrill adventures.

In summertime, Queenstown's claim-to-fame activities are the Shotover Jet Boat and the AJ Hackett's Kawarau River Bungy Jump. The Shotover Jet is a thrill-a-minute jet boat ride in a narrow river canyon just a few minute's drive north of Q-town. This jet boat operation often wins NZ awards for being a well-run highly-rated bang-for-the-buck value (see G9). AJ Hackett's Kawarau River Bungy is located a few kms east of town on the historic bridge spanning the scenic Kawarau River. Even if you have no intention of jumping, seeing the bungying is a MUST. It's easy to watch and photograph from either the actual bridge or the immense view-platform. Nobody should visit Queenstown without popping in to see the World's first commercial bungy jump!

Q8 > QUEENSTOWN HILL WALKWAY

EPIC VIEWS DIRECTLY ABOVE QUEENSTOWN

Walk: moderate 90-minute (5km) semi-loop
- elevation trailhead: 420m
- elevation peak: 820m
- bring: Botticelli model

OBSCURE   POPULAR

OBSCUR-O-METER

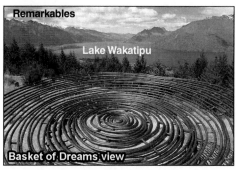

Remarkables

Lake Wakatipu

Basket of Dreams view

Queenstown Hill is the town's signature viewpoint walk, for those not inclined to pay for a Gondola view. A map-board at the carpark shows the route. This semi-loop is a steady and steep climb of switch-backs through deep forest before delivering you to the first view-point—the "*Basket of Dreams*" sculpture. This basket of views may seem like enough heavy-breathing, but the tip-top of the hill is only another 10 minutes and VERY worth it—it's Remarkablesly Better! (Even going one minute up from the *Basket* opens up a way better view.) From the peak the view is quite expansive, and, better yet, you're higher than the 790m tourist Gondola. Lake Wakatipu does its signature lightning-shaped slash around 1,978m Cecil Peak, the Remarkables pierce the skyline to the south,

and all Q-town is directly below. Bonus fun is watching airplanes swoop below you onto the airstrip. Spending a summer sunset atop Queenstown Hill is pretty nice watching the Remarkables glow red.

For a fun photo, at the *Basket of Dreams* get your gal-pal to try to imitate Botticelli's "Birth of Venus" painting, stepping to the lip of the basket. You'll have a fun "Birth of Suzie/Jenny" to remember Queenstown by. Go ahead...try!

Walk There's a map at carpark. It takes about 20 minutes to the loop junction, 15 more to the Basket of Dreams, then 10 minutes to the peak—45 minutes total up. Go counter-clockwise on the loop section.

DRIVING: **From the Queenstown downtown public carpark roundabout, go uphill on Ballarat Rd following signs for the walk...turn right then quickly left to zigzag thru the homes to the small signed carpark.**

Wanaka,Q-town,Milford

G9 ▶ SHOTOVER RIVER CANYON

WORLD FAMOUS JET-BOATING GORGE

Walk: short riverside walk

● watch YouTube: qbt-2ygxvwu
& 4ohfkwgh6L4

OBSCURE — POPULAR
OBSCUR-O-METER

Want a nice sunny riverside hang-out spot that is guaranteed to be action-packed? If so, head to the "beach" just upstream of the Shotover Jet's dock/office where you'll find some sandy spots to hang out as the Jet-boating action blazes just meters away. A Shotover Jet roars by every few minutes and a bit upstream rafts whoosh through

Shotover Office

Shotover River

the whitewater Oxenbridge river tunnel. Whoa, no lack of adrenaline on this stretch of river! Upstream at this "Oxenbridge beach" is a short track accessing the tunnel the whitewater rafts shoot through (and capsize!).

Here's an idea for some fun: make a sign that says "Splash Me", stand at the water's edge, and see if the Jet-boat pilots will oblige. Of course it'll help if you're wearing a bikini to entice the male-driven boats!! Take my word, when the Jet whooshes its tale and tosses up a 5m spray of water over you…I guarantee you'll cackle with joy!

Shotover Jet. This <u>IS</u> the most exciting boat ride ever! The World-famous Shotover Jet is 25 minutes of white-knuckle thrills. Of all the Kiwi manufactured "adventures", the Shotover Jet is THE BEST. Don't miss it. In terms of unique thrills, the other NZ Jet rides all pale in comparison. The Shotover Jet blasts through a narrow rock-bound gorge, hops rapids, and spins enough 360s to give you a face full of Shotover. Even if you're not too keen on Kiwi $$-adventures, the Shotover is worth it!

Jet ▶

Tunnel outflow

Oxenbridge Track

DRIVING: This Shotover riverside spot is directly across from the Shotover Jet office. From Q-town's corner roundabout head towards Arrowtown for 5km and then on the <u>near side</u> of the Shotover Canyon bridge turn left onto the Oxenbridge Rd for 500m to the riverside parking.

Wanaka,Q-town,Milford

G10 MT. CRICHTON LOOP TRACK

SCENIC AND HISTORIC TRACK

Walk: moderate 2-hour (8km) loop

- elevation trailhead: 350m
- elevation top: 600m

OBSCUR-O-METER
OBSCURE / POPULAR

The Mt Crichton loop is a good track because it gives you a decent workout while packing in both some scenic and historic interest. This is the most varied track in the Queenstown area. The loop, going clockwise, begins up the one-time gold-filled 12-Mile Creek. There are plenty of bridged crossings and sometimes you can still see/hear gold miners trying to find a little "flash in the pan" down in the creekbed.

Miner's cabin

Along the way you'll see a gold-sluicing tunnel and a charmingly re-habbed gold miner's cabin that's open for a historic look-see.

After the cabin comes the steeper part of the climb…but then also the payback for the sweating—nice sweeping views! Viewpoints show Lake Dispute in the wooded valley below and then a wonderful big eyeful of Lake Wakatipu and its surrounding peaks up ahead.

If the weather is cloudy this track is a good option. On a pure sunshine day it's better to head up the Remarkables Road or drive to Glenorchy.

Lake Wakatipu
Lake Dispute
Mt. Crichton Ridge

DRIVING: Head 12km west of Q-town towards Glenorchy and look for the signed carpark 1km past 12-Mile Delta.

Wanaka,Q-town,Milford

UBER-SCENIC DRIVE TO UBER-SCENIC TRACKS

Drive: 13km 2WD gravel road to Remarkables ski lodge
Walk: 2 moderate walks

• watch YouTube: wLqn3uvuw9w

OBSCUR-O-METER

This road is Remarkable[2]! First, it's the 13km gravel access road for The Remarkables ski fields. Second, it's about the highest public-access road that you can drive in NZ, ending at the 1,600m Remarkables Ski

Area Lodge—an incredible 1,300m above the lake's 308m level! And third, Tourism Q-town doesn't tell you about a FREE drive up this road as an area attraction, even though the views along the road are car-stop, jaw-drop, camera-click dazzling!

Amazingly, neither the mainstream guidebooks nor any tourist literature mentions this do-it-yourself venture. Is there no room in "Adventure-town NZ" for anything that's free?? Driving up the Remarkables in summer is definitely where Tourism Q-town <u>doesn't</u> want you—they want your butt in a Jetboat, bungy harness, 4WD tour, raft, funyak, etc etc. For do-it-yourselfers the FREE drive up the Remarkables is a must-do. You'll revel in the glories of Queenstown's true beauty as the views sweep from peaks to lakes to rivers to EVERYWHERE.

Drive The Remarkables Rd is off of SH 6 just south of Q-town and Frankton—3km south of the Kawarau River Bridge.

The views on the drive begin almost immediately up the road, but 4km up is a looping pulloff worth a first gawk. At the 6km mark there's a parking area and short path up to the 900m Trig's PHENOMENAL view, both out

Remarkables Road view

Coronet Peak Ski Field

Looking down on Shotover River

over the lake and down directly below at the confluence of the Shotover and Kawarau Rivers. You'll see the milky Shotover River actually blending with the crystalline Kawarau River, making the Kawarau a bit more opaque as it flows towards those splash-ing bungy'ers bouncing around a few kms downriver. Above the Trig the views don't dramatically improve too much, so turn back there if you don't like cliff-edge washboard road. The Lodge itself isn't too scenic, but the tracks from the lodge are. Remarkables, here you come!

Lake Alta. Lake Alta is a small turquoise teardrop of a lake nestled under the ominously jagged peaks of The Remarkables. The Lake Alta Track is just a short 30-minute one-way walk (200m ascent) up from the Remarkables Ski Lodge. The lake is a classic cirque lake filling a glacially scoured basin with the super-scenic black crags of 2,319m Double Cone towering above. From the lodge you can't see the lake's basin. Until you walk half-way up the track you'll have no idea how dramatic the view is going to be, nor how sapphire blue a lake can be.

Walk ➤ From the carpark head up and around the lodge's right side on the road. Skip the immediate right turn that heads to Shadow Basin and continue 5 minutes up the road to the next signed junction. Go right and up this steeper road. At the top of this incline, as the road turns sharply right, look for the marked track near the bog which heads up the rocky slope to the lake.

Shadow Basin Lookout. The Shadow Basin Lookout defies description—it's too good! This viewpoint is one of NZ's finest alpine views, yet it receives little-to-no publicity. A crowded day is you and a Kea. The lookout is perched at 2,000m on the jagged rocky ridge immediately below Single Cone. Surprisingly, the trek to the view is only 40-45 minutes climbing 400 vertical meters from the ski lodge, all on a ski-field "road". The island's

cont'd ➡

Double
Cone

Lake Alta

other showcase high-alpine viewpoint—Avalanche Peak at Arthur's Pass, is about the same altitude but requires an arduous 2-3 hour trek to get the view. The adjective-defying view of Shadow Basin is almost too good to be true! Not just Q-town and pretty blue Lake Wakatipu sprawling below...not just airplanes zooming the runway over the Shotover River delta, not just Coronet Peak and Ben Lomond looking like mere bumps....the MOST AMAZING aspect of this view is that, on a clear day, all of Fiordland's peaks shine! The horizon is wall-to-wall snow-capped peaks! Sight Glenorchy's 2,820m Mt Earnslaw, with its glaciered crown, directly above the Shotover bridge. Look for the pointy peak of the Milford Road's Mt Christina (rising above Lake Marian) in the distance above and just left of the Kawarau bridge. **Basically, on a clear day, this may be the most bang-for-the-buck view available any-where in New Zealand!**

Walk/Tramp From the carpark you'll be following the chairlift that runs up the steep waterfall hill to the right of the lodge. Begin around the lodge on the road and take the first right turn. This rugged "road" now goes all the way to the top of the chairlift, the first half being easy and the second half more steep and rough. Reaching the lift's top, a path begins to the left of the ski field map. It quickly zigzags through the rocks to the lookout. (FYI: it looks like the rocks to the left of the lookout might have a killer south view. They don't.)

Coming down, it's possible to skirt across the northern ridge on the ski road and then rock-hop down to the pond/ski lift to make a loop.

Watch killer YouTube vids:
(Lake Alta)
dmuadomdj1e

(Shadow Lookout)
mj9uqs8vygq

Shadow Basin Lookout Panorama

Wanaka,Q-town,Milford

G12 › ROUTEBURN TRACK DAY WALK
THE GLENORCHY SIDE OF THE FAMED ROUTEBURN

Walk: moderate 1.5 hours (7km) one-way to Flats hut
moderate 2.5 hours (9km) one-way to Falls hut
- elevation trailhead: 470m
- elev. Flats hut 670m • elev. Falls hut: 1,000m

OBSCURE POPULAR
OBSCUR-O-METER

Mt. Earnslaw
Routeburn Valley
Glenorchy
Lake Wakatipu
Road to Heaven

First off, the 44km drive from Queenstown to Glenorchy is a must-do! It rivals the marvelous drives of Te Anau/Milford and Lake Pukaki/Mt Cook. The road hugs the shore of blue-blue Lake Wakatipu with the high peaks of the Ailsa Range to the left and huge glaciated Mt Earnslaw rising above the twin valleys of the Dart and Rees rivers directly ahead at Glenorchy. Gorgeous-a-rama! (Watch YouTube: 1ktijhpgpzs)

Routeburn Swingbridge

The Routeburn "Great Walk" begins 26km north of Glenorchy, north of both the Rees and Dart River bridges. For a day walk on the famed Routeburn Track there are two good options—long and longer. The long day-walk is to the Routeburn Flats Hut, which is located in a meadowed valley amidst sky-scraping peaks. This walk is a gradual 200m ascent over 7km distance, most all the walk through a thick Beech forest. Views are limited the entire way, but there are a few swing bridges with some minor views and the emerald Routeburn River accompanies most of the track. My personal opinion is that this route is a bit dull and the "payoff" views at the Flats hut isn't huge for the 1.5-hour one-way walk. But....

If you have the energy and fitness, the next 45-minute climb to the Routeburn Falls Hut (330m ascent) makes the longer day-walk option exceptionally worthwhile! Shortly after the Flats hut the track steepens

Carpark (7km)

Flats Hut →

Track view on the way to falls

and the views improve dramatically. Reaching the Falls hut you'll pop above the 1,000m bushline to glorious 360° views, as well as cascading Routeburn Falls. This hut-side waterfall has plenty of waterfall pools for everyone—bring a swimsuit for the crowded hut environs. The Routeburn Falls hut has one of the best locations of any Great Walk hut in NZ—peaks, valleys, waterfalls…total ooh-la-la. Expect lots of "Great-walkers" clustered at Routeburn Falls' two busy huts.

Flats Hut →

Falls Huts →

Routeburn Falls View

A day-walk on the Routeburn allows you to sample the famous Routeburn without all the planning/$$/shuttle hassle of the "Great Walk." You can also try to pick a sunny day rather than getting stuck with whatever day you had to book. No need to pay heaps, plan heaps, and endure a night's stay with the 70-odd people packing the two huts at the site. Gotta love great free NZ day-walks!

Walk ▶ Straightforward walk with signs the entire route and a detailed mapboard at the carpark. Round-trip to the Falls hut and back is about 5 hours—an 18km, 600m vertical gain.

DRIVING: The road to Routeburn is signed from Glenorchy. It's 26km from Glenorchy, beautiful the entire way, the last 10km gravel. Stop on the Dart River bridge and you may see a Jetboat roar under you!

TE ANAU'S BEST DAY WALK

Walk: easy one-hour (5km) one-way

- elevation trailhead: 190m
- elevation lake: 180m

OBSCURE POPULAR
OBSCUR-O-METER

Shallow Bay
Lake Manapouri

The scenic final stretch of the Kepler "Great Walk" makes for a super easy and pleasant day-walk. This one-hour slice of the 3-4 day Kepler Track leaves from the Rainbow Reach carpark, quickly crosses a long swingbridge over the Waiau River, then ambles through dense forest over to the shore of Lake Manapouri. Everything about this easy track is low-key beautiful. The beautiful track surface is flat and wide—good for long conversations, as there's no heavy-breathing the entire route. The beautiful Beech forest is silent except for singing birds and chirping cicadas. The forest features both an endless undulating carpet of lush green moss and an open under-story enabling you to see deep into the woods. And then, for a nice finale, you get the beautiful Lake Manapouri beaches with a backdrop of snow-capped Fiordland mountains.

Lush forest,
easy walking

Wanaka,Q-town,Milford

Waiau River Bridge

Nearing the lake you come to a junction and a choice to make to head either to the Moturau Hut along the Kepler Track or the Shallow Bay Hut on a dead-end spur track. **Choose Shallow Bay!** The Moturau Hut will probably have a heap of Kepler backpackers boisterously splashing off their trail filth, while Shallow Bay and its sandy beach will have warmer water and fewer people (few Kepler walkers will add the extra out/back length to Shallow Bay, except for hut over-nighters who tend to leave early). If you continue past the Shallow Bay hut just another 5-8 minutes along the shore you'll find even nicer sandy beaches and the mouth of the Waiau River surging into the lake. Bring picnic, sunscreen, bug spray, and birthday suit—if it's sunny you'll want to stay a while.

For either an overnight backpack trip (or a fast trail-run), this almost-flat track is perfect. There are plenty of tent sites along the shorelines of Shallow Bay. Also, if Te Anau is drizzly, the Beech forest is still very nice for a rainy-day walk.

Walk ▶ Cross the initial bridge and go left. At the next odd junction stay left. Now about 50 minutes to the beach-choice junction.

Privacy past Shallow Bay Hut

DRIVING: The Rainbow Reach carpark is signed on SH 95 half way between Manapouri and Te Anau, about 10km from each.

G14 ▶ KEY SUMMIT TRACK

360° OF JAW-DROP FIORDLAND

**Walk: moderate 45-minute (4km) one-way,
with optional extra 2km**

- elevation trailhead: 530m; summit: 919m
- watch YouTube: svau9o1mdzo

OBSCUR-O-METER

The track up to Key Summit is the most popular substantial day-walk in Fiordland, and justifiably so. The first half of the walk is on the famed Routeburn Track, beginning at "The Divide" carpark. After about 30 minutes (2.5km) on the Routeburn you'll branch off for a switchbacked ascent up to Key Summit's head-swiveling viewpoint. The track is so well-made that there are no steps—just a gradual easy-walking ascent. Popping above the bushline onto Key Summit's ridge, mountains and valleys literally stretch in every direction. A plaque points out all the visible skyline peaks and valleys, surprisingly with altitudes in feet instead of meters (NZ switched to metric in 1976...quite an old plaque). Key Summit is so-named because it's situated at the head of three different valleys, each river flowing to a different coast: the Hollyford flows north to the west coast, the Eglinton to the south coast, and the Greenstone to Queenstown's Lake Wakatipu and further the east coast. At the summit there's a short loop track touring photogenic alpine tarns and a short spur track up to a viewpoint of Lake Marian (nestled under towering 2,474m Mt Christina).

For most folks the Marian Lake viewpoint is the turn-back point. But, if it's a nice day and you want to explore this alpine Fiordland terrain a bit more to find an even better unheralded viewpoint, then find the unsigned track behind the Marian Lake viewpoint benches. This unpublicized track

Tarns

Key Summit

continues along the ridge heading south after quickly crossing a bog boardwalk. If you walk another 20-25 minutes the payoff is more than worth the extra effort. The first bit is boggy, but then the path leaves the dense bush in favor of open ridge sweeping viewscape—think "Riders of Rohan"

Mt. Christina
Lake
Reading another guidebook
Lake Marian viewpoint

gorgeous...wow! Chances are that even if there are 30 people milling about atop Key Summit, only one or two may know to venture onto this path. You'll soon pass a view of Lake Gunn down in the Eglinton Valley and continue to a rocky knob (1,100m) which finally allows a view of Lake McKellar tucked down in the Greenstone Valley. From this knob you'll be able to see three different lakes as well as the three different valleys. This is where an avid NZ Frenzier wants to be! The path continues to points unknown, but a good turn-back point is this high-point knob overlooking Lake McKellar.

Greenstone Track
Lake McKellar
Ridge high point

DRIVING: The signed Divide carpark is on the Milford Rd about 85km from Te Anau, just past Lakes Gunn and Fergus (just before the prominent 90° bend in the Milford Rd.) There's a detailed mapboard at the carpark (of course not showing bonus DOC track).

Wanaka,Q-town,Milford

187

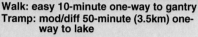

Walk: easy 10-minute one-way to gantry
Tramp: mod/diff 50-minute (3.5km) one-
way to lake

● elevation trailhead: 315m
● elevation lake: 700m

OBSCUR-O-METER

The Marian Lake Track can either be a short bang-for-the-buck pit-stop on the Milford drive or a difficult tramp to a pristine and ultra-scenic hanging cirque lake.

The entire Marian Lake Track is a difficult 3.5km-one-way tramp up through the Fiordland jungle to the shore of the jaw-drop lake. If you'd rather not do the entire tramp due to time/fitness/whatever, then the first bit of the track still makes for a great short break on the road to/from Milford. The short excursion begins with a bouncy jaunt on the swing bridge over the gin-clear Hollyford River (Bombay Sapphire Gin!) Then 7 more minutes of easy walking brings you to the "gantry" section of Marian Creek where a sweet-as suspended catwalk hugs the rock wall above the churning "Class V" rapids of the creek for a couple hundred meters. The second gantry is your turn-back point for a short outing.

For trampers the track continues from the gantries about 45 more minutes to the shore of Lake Marian. (This track would suck in rainy weather…only go if it's fair weather). Marian Lake is a cirque lake nestled in a bowl under the sheer crags of Mt Christina (left) and Mt Lyttle (right). This is truly phenomenal alpine scenery! The waterfall-laden ridge on lake's left towers 1,000m straight above the lake. The track up to the lake is true

Gantry
(10-min walk)

tramping—rugged roots and rocks the entire way, but the payoff is huge. Marian Lake, despite the icy waterfalls cascading into it, invites a quick refreshing dip after the sweaty climb.

**Watch YouTube:
krkmyxtohj8
&
x6seyckk2o**

Track

Roots 'n' rocks
to Lake Marian

DRIVING: The Marian Lake carpark is signed just 1km down the Lower Hollyford Rd (3km past The Divide).

G16 ▶ HUMBOLDT FALLS ADVENTURE

SWIMMING HOLE ADVENTURING!!!!

Tramp: moderate 30-min (1.0km) rock-hop
Walk: easy 10-min track to viewpoint

• bring: backpack with camera, bug spray, beer

OBSCUR-O-METER

Oh my, this excursion is 100% NZ Frenzy…100% pure New Zealand!!!!

In Fiordland, at the end of the Lower Hollyford Rd, is a quick track leading to a viewpoint of the distant 270m Humboldt Falls. Humboldt Falls may be the highest year-round "named" waterfall that you can see for free in NZ! The other biggies—Sutherland, Brown, etc all cost $$ on the Milford Track and such. The question for travelers is, is it worth it to drive 16km of the gravel Hollyford Rd for an 8-minute stroll to see the distant Humboldt Falls, especially after driving the Milford's waterfall-laden road? No…it's not worth the long detour.

But… if you're a keen off-the-beaten-path adventurer who's ready to suit up with water shoes, swimsuit, and sandfly spray…and willing to make a fairly easy 30-minute rock-hop up Humboldt's streambed…then definitely, absolutely, 100% GO!

I don't want to ruin the surprises of this excursion, but I need to tell you enough to get you motivated to try this adventure. On the rare sunny warm day in Fiordland this adventure tops my list. That's saying a lot! Here's what you do: you put on your water shoes/sandals and rock-hop/

270m!

Viewpoint
view

splash up the Humboldt Stream from where the swingbridge crosses the stream at the beginning of the Hollyford Track. After 15 minutes you'll begin to see the gargantuan Humboldt Falls ahead—quite impressive! The stream is relatively warm because it originates as rain rather that glacial-melt. Emerald pools will have you fetching out your camera. Nearing the base of Humboldt Falls you'll find a deep swimming hole and another surprise I won't tell you about. You may have to swim the pool to get past the final rocks, but you can also clamber

Rock-hop
upstream

over the top of the right-side rocks. Shangri-La is the destination. 'Nuff said. Maybe bring a few cans of weak-ass Kiwi beer, cuz you're gonna wanna celebrate. This is what I come to NZ for, and it's surprises like this spot that make me write this kind of guidebook. Whaddaya think?? Lemme know!!

Tramp You might want to first go up the easy viewpoint track to warm up and see what's coming, but if you simply trust me and want to be surprised, then just take to the streambed and GO. Make sure to bring your bug spray with so when you swim and wash off you can re-apply. When you round the last corner at the first pool, the "easy" way is up and over the right-side rocks. If it's a rare warm Fiordland day and you don't skinny-dip…then I'll never sell you another book again!

DRIVING: Lower Hollyford Rd is 90km from Te Anau, signed 3km past The Divide. Turn and go 16km of gravel to the road-end.

FYI The Moraine Track swingbridge, just before the road-end, is <u>way</u> worth a look. (The track though…sucks.)

FIORDLAND SPLENDOR, NO TOURISTS!!!

Tramp: easy/mod 45-minute (3.5km) one-way
- elevation trailhead: 800m
- elevation valley end: 900m
- elevation saddle: 1,400m

OBSCURE / POPULAR

OBSCUR-O-METER

This shorter slice of the longer Gertrude Saddle Route is the Milford Road's little secret. (The "official" 5km DOC route to Gertrude Saddle is a serious rough-going tramping outing, gaining 500m in elevation in the final 2km). But, little-known is that the first 3.5kms of the route are

🏔 **Gertrude Saddle** ↑
3.5 km / 4-6 hr return
For fit and experienced trampers only
Unmarked route - alpine and navigation skills required

wonderfully easy and jaw-drop gorgeous along the almost-flat Gertrude Valley floor, before encountering the lung-busting headwall ascent. The 45-minute walk described here follows DOCs markers up the valley floor to the snowfield at the base of the sheer Gertrude headwall.

The Gertrude Valley, as seen from the road, is impressive…but when you enter into its embrace, the road sounds replaced by 500m waterfall gurgle, the sheer ramparts so high it's impossible to both look upwards and walk at the same time…ahh yes, the Gertrude becomes superlative! As you approach the headwall the U-shape of the glacial gouge becomes more pronounced. Waterfalls tumble all around and the small snow field at the valley's end beckons you onwards. You can turn back whenever you feel like it, but getting to and sitting atop the valley-end snowfield with waterfalls roaring into the abyss at your back is phenomenal. WOW, Fiordland splendor minus the tourist hordes! Looking back down the valley, tourist cars whiz by in the distance, never knowing that **there is one easy, uncrowded track that gets you out of the car and into the heart-stopping glory of Fiordland!**

Also, unlike the Key Summit or Marian Lake tracks, this is a great excursion no matter what the weather.

Walk/Tramp ▶ Begin past the DOC sign at the carpark following DOCs markers. Half way up the valley the route fades and the markers disappear, but a route towards the waterfall-laden headwall is somewhat marked by rock-stack cairns. Or, just pick your way up the rocky streambed to the obvious headwall snow field. Left of the snow field the Gertrude Saddle Route heads steeply upwards (consult with DOC in Te Anau for maps/current conditions/advice info before attempting the difficult headwall tramp.)

Gertrude
Saddle

Waterfall ice field

Route

Ice field
waterfall

DRIVING: Gertrude Valley is signed on the Milford Road 11km past Lower Hollyford Rd and 1.5km east of Homer Tunnel. There's a private hut near the carpark, but don't head towards it, but rather follow the DOC pointers for the route.

TUNNEL-MOUTH ICE ADVENTURE WITH KEA PARROTS

Tramp: 70m of cool!

- elevation tunnel: 900m
- watch YouTube: uwuerwaw-e4 & 1kyq5nLge-i

OBSCUR-O-METER

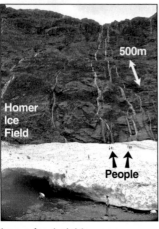

500m

Homer
Ice
Field

↑↑
People

Homer Tunnel pierces Fiordland's craggy peaks on the drive to Milford Sound. The Homer Tunnel is one of the most impressive road engineering feats on the South Island. The tunnel has stoplights on either side to regulate the one-way traffic. You'll often have to stop and wait to get through the tunnel…but this is a GOOD THING, as this is jaw-drop Fiordland territory!

At the Tunnel's east side you'll find sky-scraping peaks laced with waterfalls pouring down into a roadside snow field. Kea parrots flutter about the scene. People play atop the snow field. The impressive glacier-like snow field often has a fog-belching snow cave at its foot. Heaps of people walk down to take a photo at the snow-cave entrance, but few dare to set foot inside.

For some silly reason people think walking atop the snowfield is safe, whereas walking into it would be dangerous. This beckoning snowfield cave is a WAY safer place than the Milford Road, but tourists seem afraid of it. Go figure.

If you're in NZ for some true natural adventure, then lace-up the sandals, roll up the pant legs and in you go for an odyssey of wonders! The cave is only

Inside the ice tunnel

about 70m long, but dark and foggy enough to need a good flashlight. A waterfall often pours into the upstream end of the cave. Upon re-emerging out of the ice cave after a 5-minute look-see, you'll smirk at the gaggle of snap-happy tourists who'll look at you like some phantom of the ice. Shake

Kea at Homer Tunnel

your head at their timidity, shoo the Keas off your path, then continue on to find more of Fiordland's amazing amazing-ness. Hurry, you're in a frenzy!

FYI > Across the road there's a DOC track that escapes the tourists to explore the sights 'n' snowfields on that side of the tunnel.

Wanaka,Q-town,Milford

194

DISAPPEARING RIVER!

Walk: easy 15-minute loop
Tramp: difficult one-minute adventure

• watch YouTube: weLnfnjm-8u & eqjufwwtn6e

OBSCUR-O-METER

The Chasm is a 15-minute must-see on every Fiordland tour bus itinerary. Gobs of tourists pour out onto the cemented wheelchair-access path, cameras clicking before their feet hit the ground. Sounds crappy? Surprisingly, it's not…honestly!

The Chasm is best to visit when you're leaving Milford—the parade of mid-day buses may have passed, and your excitement to finally see the uber-famed Milford Sound will have been quenched, so you won't be in such a hurry.

Unlike most NZ "gorges" and "chasms"…this Chasm definitely lives up to its name!! The somewhat mellow-flowing Cleddau River literally turns on its side and knifes through a swiss cheese of crazed rock sculpturing. The suddenly-pinched river roars in surprise as it plunges into a dark abyss. Impressive! On the track there are two bridges that span the

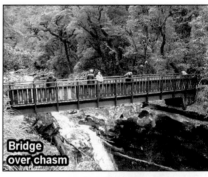

Bridge over chasm

best bits of the Chasm, and for most tourists these two bridges are the quick photo-ops before they hurry back to the bus for the rest of the descent to Milford.

But wait…if you know cameras, know waterfalls, and know what tripod, f-stop, and polarized mean…then by god make sure you take the slick rough path down past Peter's grave marker (past the two bridges on a counter-clock loop) to the boulder-top photo-perch! This is where the Chasm <u>really chasms</u>! This is where NZ Frenzy hangs out. Be super careful if it's wet out, as you don't want to be the next "Peter"!

Chasm keyhole

Scramble viewpoint

DRIVING: The Chasm is signed 8km past the Homer Tunnel, 11km before the Sound.

Wanaka,Q-town,Milford

FABLED FIORDLAND MUST-SEE

Walk: short foreshore walkway—that's it

• bring: bug spray, $$, patience, excitement

OBSCUR-O-METER

Milford Sound is home to the South Island's most iconic image—Mitre Peak towering over the Sound. Every NZ traveler is told that a cruise on either Milford or Doubtful Sound is a Fiordland Natl Park MUST. Fewer have been told that the drive to the Sound is probably a greater visual highlight than a cruise on either Sound. Milford is all tourist hustle-bustle, whereas Doubtful is quieter and more expensive.

Mitre Peak

Stirling Falls (150m)

What you shouldn't do is take the Doubtful cruise and skip the drive on the Milford Road! The 120km drive from Te Anau to Milford Sound is a marvel…a visual cornucopia of delight…a smorgasbord of oooh and ahhhs and neck-craning magnificence!! Undoubtedly it's one of the FINEST DRIVES in the WORLD! After a so-so start along hard-to-see Lake Te Anau, the mountains begin to rise up as the Eglinton Valley narrows. You'll think the first 85km to The Divide are pretty WOW…but then, once you drop to the Hollyford River…the next 32km are adjective defying. Sheer-sided mountains pierce the clouds, craggy snow peaks reign all around while multi-thousand-foot waterfalls decorate every visible rock face. Once through the Homer Tunnel the visuals never cease until you pull into the carpark with a front 'n' center view of mile-high Mitre Peak crowning Milford Sound!

Once at Milford, of course you'll take a boat ride—it is worth it simply to escape Milford's ever-present plague of sandflies. Surprisingly though, the best view of Milford is from the foreshore walkway, not the cruise boats. Most all the boats do the same route, all pulling close-in to 150m Stirling Falls for a misty drenching, all pulling close to the Fur Seal rock.

Wanaka,Q-town,Milford

Other than the cruise boats (or a kayak trip), there's little to do at the Sound. The quick Foreshore walk is a must for photographers, especially to slow the shutter for 160m Bowen Falls. The Lodge is worth a look simply for its historic photos.

Camping on the Milford Rd:

There are numerous cheap-as DOC sites along the road through Eglinton Valley—each basic with no water or showers. The best of the bunch is Cascade Creek where there's plenty of space, fire-rings, good mountain views and lots of wildflowers. The Lake Gunn lakeside campsite may sound good, but this site is too small and too many people try to pack in…often arriving late at night and causing undue commotion. Skip Lake Gunn, you'll be better off at Cascade Creek!

Down the gravel Lower Hollyford Rd 8km is Gunn's Hollyford campground. It's a regular family campground, but friendlier…for just $10pp. Hot showers, kitchen, the works…and possibly a big fire burning in the camp area—very social! Gunn's shop has some groceries as well as books, maps, and souvenirs. This is a fabulous campground!

The Milford Sound Lodge, at the Sound, has some camping but VERY limited and most often sold-out. About $20pp, but you better book ahead.

Mile-high Mitre Peak (1,692m)

Wanaka,Q-town,Milford

SANDFLIES

Beware!

Sandflies on the South Island's West Coast and Fiordland are HORRID. No two ways about it…they are awful and will drive you mad within a week!! In my opinion travelers aren't given enough warning about the West Coast sandfly plague because Tourism doesn't want to discourage visitation. But this is what happens: travelers, either fresh from Chch or coming down from the North Island, have been lulled into a false sense of security about the upcoming swarm. Neither Chch nor the entire North Island suffers the swarming plague that awaits West Coast travelers. Thus, travelers are often caught unawares and without the necessary bucket-o-DEET. One hour of exposed skin in Sandfly country and you'll have a legion of hyper-itchy bumps on your ankles (especially) that will bother you for the rest of your South Island trip. You need to be prepared with Deet <u>BEFORE</u> you get to Sandfly country!!!!! The sandflies around Abel Tasman are only a wee taste of the upcoming nightmare. Get DEET and put it on before dusk comes, as these vampires feast at dusk, not night!!!

Finally, after a journey down the West Coast, often itching all the way and losing patience for this "why didn't they tell me" plague, you'll pop over Haast Pass and leave the sandfly swarm behind when you get to Wanaka. This is why EVERYONE LOVES Wanaka's beach—because you can finally lay down without swatting!! Queenstown is relatively sandfly free also, but once in Te Anau…be prepared for another cursed onslaught. Fiordland

Sandfly swarm on tent

can be the worst in NZ, but too bad they don't tell Milford track walkers that. FYI, at Milford Sound, you will be devoured as you exit your car, but once on a boat...no more sand-flies, as they can't keep up.

Also, all three South Island highway mountain passes are sandfly nightmares.

Here's what Capt Cook had to say about NZ's pestilence...and this is from a guy who sailed filthy ships around the world, before Deet was even a dream:

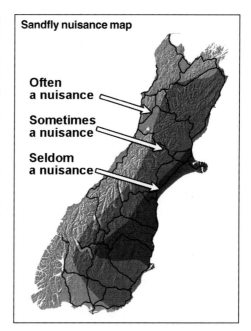

Sandfly nuisance map

Often a nuisance

Sometimes a nuisance

Seldom a nuisance

Captain Cook's 1773 journal reads, in reference to Fiordland:

'The most mischievous animal here is the small black sandfly which are exceeding numerous and are so troublesome that they exceed everything of the kind I ever met with, wherever they light they cause a swelling and such intolerable itching that it is not possible to refrain from scratching and at last ends in ulcers like the small Pox."

Here's a summation: Sandflies are most active at dawn and dusk, and on grey days—they don't like direct hot sun, nor do they fly or bite in the dark. Sandflies can't deal with either wind or rain. Sandflies fly very slowly, and thus if you are walking, they can't keep up, thus, keep moving, no sandflies....if you slow down, YIKES!

Sandflies, unlike mosquitoes, are silent assassins. They land and bite without you hearing or feeling them, especially around your ankles. <u>Wearing long pants and socks is the best prevention</u>—the ankles are where they bite you the worst!!!

<u>When</u> you get bit, if you're hyper-sensitive, then pop into the pharmacy for some anti-itch cream...but don't expect miracles. The best thing to do is to prepare yourself for the sandfly attack by hosing yourself down with Deet, and then laughing as you watch the less-prepared tourists. hahahahaha

PENGUIN-A-RAMA

Watch *Meet the Locals*:
"Hoiho" and "Yellow-eyed Penguins"

Yellow-eyed Penguins are one of the world's rarest penguin species with a worldwide population estimated at just 4,000 penguins, with less than 1,000 nesting on mainland NZ. They are often cited as "The world's rarest penguins". These YEPs were recently granted Endangered Species protections (Aug 2010).

Surprisingly, Yellow-eyed Penguins are fairly easy to find along the SE coast of the South Island, from Oamaru south through the Catlins, if you both where to look and when to look. Seeing penguins in NZ is often a highlight of travelers' trips, especially since most folks will never have a chance anywhere else on the planet to see wild penguins. Don't miss the chance – you'll love the waddle and hop! (Personally, I had thought, "what's the big deal about seeing penguins?", but once I saw some, I was hooked! They are captivating to watch!!)

Here are some insights about spotting YEPs:

1) They come ashore a little before dusk—think 5-8pm in summer.
2) They waddle ashore, often preen and dry a bit, then waddle into the bushes/grasses and make their way to often far-off unseen nest sites.
3) "Hides" are built at various beaches to view the penguins from. Bring binoculars. These hides are wooden cabins with slot-like windows that open for beach viewing…thus, you can see the penguins, but they can't see you.

Here's some author opinion:

The two best places to see YEPs are at <u>Curio Bay</u> and <u>Moeraki's Katiki Pt.</u>

Curio Bay receives little publicity, but it's the best. Only at Curio can you sit and watch the penguins march past you just meters away, while you can take all the pictures you want…no binoculars needed! DOC stations a very-visible volunteer ranger at the site to ensure good behavior and answer questions. Curio's penguins seem habituated to human presence (unlike the other "Hide" locations), so they'll march right on past you, and once in the brush they often sound off and screech. U N F O R G E T T A B L E ! ! ! YouTube "Curio Bay Penguins" to see some action.

Moeraki's Katiki Pt features a Hide, but also a lesser-known track that heads over the hill from the lighthouse towards the point. Amazingly, along this track you may spot penguins just meters away, even in broad daylight!! Sometimes in the middle of the afternoon you'll find YEPs marching to and fro up/down the hillsides. Incredible!! Check YouTube video # L1bk4iz0e8w (YappyHappyZipper) for some amazing footage.

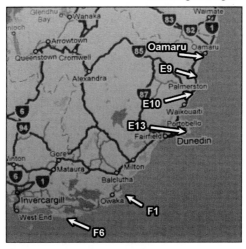

Scott Cook's "penguin-watch best bets"

Curio Bay petrified tidal shelf (F6)
Moeraki's Katiki Pt Hide and Lighthouse Pt track (E9)
Dunedin's Otago Peninsula Sandfly Bay Hide (E13)
Oamaru's Bushy Beach Hide
Nugget Point Lighthouse's Roaring Bay Hide (F1)
Shag Pt View platform (E10)

Commercial Penguin viewing:

Oamaru's Blue Penguin Colony. (www.penguins.co.nz). About $25-30 for nighttime viewing grandstand admission. Here you can sit and watch Blue penguins come ashore en masse, with subdued lighting from the grandstand.

Dunedin Otago Peninsula's *Penguin Place.* (www.Penguinplace.co.nz). About $35 for 90-minute tour with guaranteed sightings and photography. A private landowner has made his property super penguin-friendly, as well as tourist-friendly, and they've won numerous con-servation awards by doing so.

Appendix 3 FUR SEALS vs. SEA LIONS

Watch *Meet the Locals*:
"NZ Fur Seal" and "Sea Lions"

Fur Seal colonies are the most prevalent and you'll see Fur Seals all around the South Island. Sea Lions, on the other hand, are all just at the very southern tip of the island, mostly Dunedin south through the Catlins.

Though the animals look similar, their behavior on land towards humans is vastly different. Put simply, Sea Lions are like Scooby-Doo, whereas Fur Seals are more Rottweiler-like. In a way you can compare them to sheep and cows. Like sheep, seals don't much like humans and they run away. They're wary and often bolt for the sea when surprised or when you walk between them and the sea. To contrast, Sea Lions act more like cows—they don't seem bothered by humans and are sometimes curious to come closer. Most often Sea Lions don't care if you walk around them or between them and the sea. Sea Lions often seem big and goofy, curious and playful when on land (when they're not just lying comatosely flicking sand up on themselves.) As the DOC literature puts it, "Sea Lions are generally quite confident around people." One time at Curio Bay in the Catlins there were two young Sea lion males wrestling with each other <u>against</u> a tourist camper-van—they were shaking the van as they bashed each other and the tourist inside was peeking out the window in abject horror—hilarious! Another time at Sandfly Bay in Dunedin a Sea lion came up to lie down in front of the "Hide" door—a long way up from the sea—where he marched around huffing and comically chasing at the frightened penguin-watchers. It seemed he just wanted a bit of fun chasing people back and forth.

Sea Lion

Fur Seals though, now they're a different story. In my many lonely beach walks I would often surprise upon some seals as they hid-out in the shady nooks behind beach rocks…and when I surprised them they would wake with a terrifying roar and snarl, scaring the begeezus out of me! I quickly learned that when walking near rocks on lonely coastlines to yell

Fur Seal

out and clap a bit to wake up any seals that may be hidden behind rocks...sort of like making noise when walking through Canadian bear country. Never did a seal ever come close to attacking me, but wow, what an adrenaline rush to have a wild bull roar up just meters away! The seals at Kaikoura's Kean Point are fairly accustomed to humans and let bad human behavior slide, but if you get near a wilder one—watch out! Once at sea though, the young seals can be delightfully playful "in their element." I totally recommend the "Seal Swim" tours (Kaikoura, Abel Tasman, etc). The more playful and curious you are the more curious and playful they become—if you're a confident swimmer the experience will be unforgettable!

To tell a Fur Seal from a Sea Lion isn't easy until you've seen plenty. Fur Seals have pointier noses and longer whiskers. Sea Lions are bigger and look more blubbery. Seals recline on rocks, Sea Lions on sand (this is often the best tell-tale). If you are near one and making noise...and it isn't bothered...then it's a Sea Lion. If you're north of Moeraki or anywhere on the West Coast, then chances are it's a Fur Seal.

New Zealand's seals: what's the difference?

New Zealand sea lions
- Males: 350–500 kg; brown/black.
- Females: 100–160 kg, cream/silver.
- Blunt nose, short whiskers.
- Found on sandy beaches and surrounds.

Male (left) and female (right) sea lions
Photo: Rod Morris

New Zealand fur seals
- Males: 90–150 kg; dark brown.
- Females: 30–50 kg; dark brown.
- Pointy nose, long whiskers.
- Found on rocky coastlines.

Sub-adult male sea lion
Photo: Karen Baird

The Kea. (Key-a) The Kea is one of the world's only alpine parrots and is known in NZ as "The Clown of the Mountains." These cheeky, curious, smart, playful parrots are unmistakable once you've seen one. They have a dull green iridescent coloring with some orange visible under the wings when they fly.

The Kea

Keas are easily found throughout the Southern Alps areas and also around sea level at FJ/Fox Glaciers. Good spots for Keas are Homer Tunnel (G18), Arthur's Pass (B9-13), and Rob Roy Glacier (G6).

Any Google search will yield heaps of videos, the best being Animal Planet's "Kea: The Smartest Parrot" (YouTube it), and TV NZ Meet The Locals "Kea".

The Pukeko

The Pukeko. (Poo-kecko) The Pukeko is one of NZ's strangest looking birds, common throughout both islands. Pukekos are gangly looking with shiny blue-purple feathers and a bright red beak and legs. These birds are swamp hens, and thus they like damp areas to forage. Like Keas and Wekas, Pukekos are fairly undisturbed by humans as they peck about in an ever-searching look for food.

YouTube "Pukeko" to see lots of vids.

The Weka. (Weck-a) The Weka is a brown chicken-sized bird with a straight pointy beak. They're common to the forested northwestern areas of the South Island. Punakaiki's Pancake Rocks are the surest place to look for Wekas, as they commonly patrol the carparks looking for scraps. Wekas seem completely unafraid of humans, so fear not.

The Weka

The Shag

The Shag. (Yeah baby yeah) Common sea bird known worldwide as a Cormorant. You'll see them on Abel Tasman beaches and a large breeding colony at Dunedin's Taiaroa Head.

The Moa

Okarito Brown Kiwi. Only at Okarito (D6). Watch TVNZ Meet the Locals "Rarest Kiwi."

The Moa. Hunted to extinction by early Maoris. A brilliant display of various skeletons is at the Otago Museum in Dunedin.

When you see the Southern Cross for the first time, you understand now why you came this way." *Crosby, Stills and Nash*

Van window
S.Cross &
Pointers

Travelers arriving from the Northern Hemisphere will see the Southern Cross immediately upon entering New Zealand, as it's emblazoned upon the ever-present NZ flag. Better yet, once you get away from Auckland's lights, you'll have an entirely new Southern Hemisphere starscape to ponder. No more Big Dipper circling the North Star, now you've got the Southern Cross rotating a wide arc around the Southern Celestial pole. Once found, the four stars making the diamond-shape of the Southern Cross are easy to recognize, especially with the help of the Alpha and Beta Centauri, known as the two bright "Pointers".

Another immediate oddity to the nighttime NZ sky are the Magellanic Clouds. These two smallish hazy "clouds" are located somewhat to the right of the Southern Cross. You may think that they're actually nighttime sky clouds, but nope, they're actually the Milky Way's closest neighboring galaxies, resembling li'l round mini-Milky Ways (more like Almond Joys).

Gamma Crucis

Delta Crucis

Beta Crucis

Alpha Crucis

Beta Centauri

Alpha Centauri

Rigel

Orion

Betelgeuse

To the north in the sky, directly opposite of the Southern Cross is our Northern Hemisphere constellation friend, Orion. But in the NZ sky Orion is "upside down", standing on his head with his sword sticking up off the 3-star belt rather than hanging down. If you lay down and look backwards, Orion may appear as you've seen him before.

INDEX

Hope you liked my book!
Please review it on Amazon.com when you get home.